Outside

First edition 2014
Text copyright © Maria Ana Peixe Dias and Inês Teixeira do Rosário
Illustrations copyright © Bernardo P. Carvalho

The right of Maria Ana Peixe Dias, Inês Teixeira do Rosário, and Bernardo P. Carvalho to be identified as the authors and illustrator of this work has been asserted by them in accordance with the Copyright, Designs and Patents Act, 1988 (United Kingdom).

Published with the permission of Planeta Tangerina
Rua das Rosas, n.° 20, Alto dos Lombos, 2775-683 Carcavelos, Portugal

Funded by the Dirção-Geral do Livro, dos Arquivos e das Bibliotecas/Portugal

GOVERNO DE **PORTUGAL** | SECRETÁRIO DE E
DA CULTURA

DIREÇÃO-GERAL DO LIVRO, DOS ARQUIV
DAS BIBLIOTECAS

This paperback edition first published in Great Britain in 2018 by Lincoln Children's Books,
6 Blundell Street N79BH
QuartoKnows.com
Visit our blogs at QuartoKnows.com

A catalogue record for this book is available from the British Library.

ISBN 978-1-78603-161-7

Designed by Planeta Tangerina
Translated by Lucy Greaves
Original edition edited by Isabel Minhós Martins and Carlos Grifo Babo
English language edition edited by Jenny Broom

Natural history consultancy:
Ana Francisco, Sérgio Chozas and Paulo Cardoso – SPBotânica ("Flowers")
Maria João Pereira ("Mammals")
Mário Boieiro (animals and "Bugs and Critters")
Miguel Lecoq, Paulo Catry, Ricardo Tomé ("Birds")
Nuno Pedroso ("Follow The Clues" and "Mammals")
Ricardo Calado ("Beaches, Oceans, and Tidepools")
Rui Rebelo ("Amphibeans" and "Reptiles")
Sónia Anton ("The Stars, the Moon and the Sun")
Teresa Leal Rosa ("Clouds, Wind and Rain")
Teresa Melo ("Rocks")

Printed in China

9 8 7 6 5 4 3 2 1

OUTSIDE

EXPLORING NATURE

Maria Ana Peixe Dias
Inês Teixeira Do Rosário
Bernardo P. Carvalho

Translated by Lucy Greaves

Lincoln
Children's Books

Us and nature . . . a long story

Imagine people in prehistoric times, before there were villages or cities. Nature was all around them! Back then, there were no paved roads, no houses, and no electricity. There were plains stretching as far as the eye could see, rivers running freely, huge mountains and cliffs, lots of animal species (buzzing or growling ferociously), and trees and more trees.

For thousands and thousands of years, it was just us and nature.

And, in fact, there was no real separation—us on one side; plants, animals, and rivers on the other. We were so close because we depended on the natural world to survive: we needed the fruits and berries that grew on the trees; the fish that swam in the rivers and seas; the animals, large and small, that we hunted on land.

Nature was mysterious. We were starting to figure some things out, but still, everything happened as if by magic. (And there are so many mysteries left to solve today, so just imagine what it must have been like back then . . .)

Nature was also powerful. No one could hold back a raging river by force. There was no way to predict a storm. There weren't any inventions to help with farming.

Nature was a friend, but also an enemy. Imagine what it would be like to live surrounded by animals that wanted to eat you! Or what it would be like to live through hard winters, droughts, floods, and diseases that could destroy the plants you needed to eat. That's why, at the beginning, we prayed to the mountains, the trees, and the rivers. Nature was like a living person, or like a god that people could talk to and ask for things from or offer a gift to in exchange for a big favor.

l to thee, O Nile!
Thou showest thyself in this land,
Coming in peace, giving life to Egypt!

The ancient Egyptians used to sing this hymn to the Nile River.

Giving life to all animals;
Watering the land without ceasing:
The way of heaven descending:
Lover of food, bestower of corn.

Unpredictability has always scared us. The ancient Egyptians, for example, could never be sure whether or not the flooding of the Nile would water the earth and give them fertile ground. Throughout our history, the need to survive (in this case, to eat!) made us want to control nature and its forces.

We have tried to do so in many ways: by carefully observing nature, by studying its changes over time, by discovering similarities and differences, and by identifying the beings that surround us. We also used technology to make things easier, inventing more and more sophisticated tools.

As time went by, our relationship with the natural world began to change: we stopped being so afraid, and we no longer felt a need to communicate with nature or to thank it. Because nature became more or less under our control, we could use it to our advantage without worrying about the consequences.

After making a lot of mistakes, we learned that the planet has a limited capacity for renewal and also that everything on Earth is connected. If we destroy forests too quickly, they will end up disappearing completely. If we destroy the habitat of an animal, it will be in danger of extinction. If one species disappears, others will disappear. Everything works in a cycle, and we are a part of this cycle.

We try to deny it, but we are completely dependent on the planet and its resources. And, right now, nature is also dependent on us: we've become so powerful that we're capable of destroying a whole planet. And that's scary.

In spite of everything, we believe that humans have common sense. We didn't write this book out of panic that the planet would cease to exist; we wrote it with the conviction that the more we know, the better informed we are, and the more able we will be to appreciate and conserve the beauties and riches of the natural world.

Also, our experience tells us that contact with nature does us good. Spending time outside is relaxing and fun. It can make us more free and creative, more attentive and confident.

There are days when we feel like we don't have any energy, and other days when we feel like we have too much. In both cases, getting a bit of fresh air and getting close to nature can be all we need to feel better.

Where to go?

As we've already said, you can explore nature even in your backyard or the bit of land behind your house. In just trying to answer a simple question—how many different species of animals live here?—can provide a big enough challenge to keep you researching for a year. You might also just like to enjoy yourself without "scientific goals": try looking at the clouds, feeling the wind, climbing a tree, drawing flowers . . . You can do that almost anywhere!

Outside–inside cities

There are lots of species associated with urban areas. There are pigeons, sparrows, and sea gulls, of course, but if you pay a little more attention you'll likely see bats and birds of prey right in the city (like kestrels, which make their nests in tall buildings). These are just a few examples—and there are hundreds of others.

Outside–out of the cities

If you want to go on a bigger adventure, you can try to get to know a certain landscape or biotope. Outside of big cities we can find very different landscapes, some of which are very interesting from a natural point of view (especially when it comes to the variety of animals and plants).

Here are some of the most important places to explore:
Woods and forests

Forests and woods are always special places to visit, for their beauty, but also for the quantity and diversity of animals and plants that exist there. You'll certainly be able to see (and especially hear!) lots of birds singing and, if you're lucky, even hear a woodpecker "drumming" on a tree. If you look carefully, you'll see that tree trunks are covered with small insects, spiders and webs, mushrooms, lichens, and many other living things. Each tree is a forest and, in fact, a habitat in itself!

If you are visiting a forest, wood or scrubland, check out the following chapters before you go: *The Things Animals Leave Behind; Bugs and Critters; Amphibians; Trees; Birds; Reptiles; Flowers,* and *Mammals.*

Relevant chapters if you are exploring a mountain: *The Things Animals Leave Behind; Bugs and Critters; Trees; Birds; Reptiles; Flowers; Mammals; Rocks; The Stars, the Moon, and the Sun* and *Clouds, Wind, and Rain.*

Most forests that we can visit have already been altered in some way by humans—for the production of wood or charcoal, for example. Some have even been planted on purpose to be commercially exploited. Native forests (i.e. with trees that exist naturally in the region) are generally richer in fauna and flora. The most common types of forest are conifer (such as pine forests) and broadleaf (such as oak forests).

Oak forests, for example, are native forests that used to cover a huge area. They mostly contain oaks, of course, but there can be other trees too, such as beech and birch. All these trees are deciduous (in other words, they lose their leaves in the coldest months). This is why oak forests change a lot with the rhythm of the seasons—what you'll find in spring will certainly be different to autumn. Notice how the dry leaves that have fallen to the forest floor can hide a lot of surprises! Old fallen trunks also deserve special attention—you'll no doubt see mushrooms and lots of critters.

Mountains

Who's ever been up a mountain? It's definitely a unique feeling, getting to the very top! The landscape is often breathtaking, and, when we see the view for miles around, we can't help but think, "Yes! It was worth it!"

Climbing a mountain, or even just walking around the hills and valleys of a mountainous area, is almost always a guaranteed good day out. Lots of animals have adapted to live in these areas—birds are, as a general rule, the easiest to see (you'll likely see crows and birds of prey), but a closer look can reveal the odd mammal as well, and of course lots of flowers, if you go in spring. Keep an eye out for what you might find swimming in a mountain lake, too.

You'll notice that the highest parts of mountains don't usually have vegetation. This can be because the original forest has already been cut down, but in the highest mountains the most probable cause is the cold. As the altitude increases, the climatic conditions become harsher: the temperature gradually decreases, and the wind gets stronger. This is why few species are able to survive in the highest mountains.

Beaches, oceans, and islands

Most of the time, when we go to the seaside in summer, we don't always remember that beaches are very rich in fauna (this is the place where sea and land meet, and so both species that live in the water or on land can be found here). On rocky beaches we can look for starfish, mussels, and crabs, and on sandy beaches you might find clams that live buried in the wet sand, and sandpipers that flit away from the waves as they hunt for the clams . . . And this is only what we see with our feet on dry land! With goggles and flippers we can discover a whole underwater world.

Islands are also very special places. Because they're surrounded by the sea, many of the animals that live there are unable to leave and so they evolve in isolation, giving rise to new species. This is why, on islands, there are usually lots of endemic species (species that don't exist anywhere else). This happens more frequently on remote islands, i.e. the ones that are furthest from the coast. On islands we can also find important colonies of marine birds.

Rivers, estuaries, and lakes

Wetlands such as rivers, estuaries, lakes, lagoons, and swamps, are some of the places where we can spot the most species of animals and plants. We'll see more birds than anything

- - - - - - - - - - - -

If you are visiting any of these sites, read these chapters first: The Things Animals Leave Behind; Birds; Mammals; Oceans, Beaches, and Tide Pools, and The Stars the Moon, and the Sun.

- - - - - - - - - - - -

Most relevant chapters: Bugs and Critters; Amphibians; Birds; Reptiles; Mammals; Oceans, Beaches, and Tide Pools, and Clouds, Wind, and Rain.

else (there can be thousands of them), but also lots of amphibians. With a bit of luck you might see a mammal, such as an otter or beaver. There are lots of fish, of course, but they're obviously not so easy to observe. Insects are also abundant—dragonflies, water striders and many more.

Arable land and pasture

Lots of animals are interested in the places we humans cultivate. This is because many of them like the food we grow—whether cereals, vegetables or fruits—and therefore they choose these places to feed or make their nests. Other animals simply like living underneath cultivated land, where they can dig their tunnels more easily—this is the case with moles.

Before you go to a field, read the following chapters: *The Things Animals Leave Behind; Bugs and Critters; Amphibians; Trees; Birds; Reptiles; Flowers; Mammals; Rocks; The Stars the Moon, and the Sun*, and *Clouds, Wind, and Rain*.

Important things to know

Getting to know the natural world can be a fantastic experience, but there are certain things you should know to avoid dangerous situations.

Don't forget the following rules:

On trips to the country, you should always be accompanied by an adult or have their permission. And never go out alone. It will be safer; plus, if you've got company, you can always ask questions (or show them what you already know!).

Take advantage of nice days.
Sometimes you want to walk in the rain or feel the wind in your hair, but don't go outside in a storm, especially a thunderstorm. You can always admire the lightning from your window, inside your nice and cozy house.

Whether you're going to see the stars or amphibians, or hear owls singing, if you go out at night, remember that it's easy to get lost or trip on something. Always take a flashlight and a coat.

Pay attention to the path you take, especially when you're walking through a forest. It's very easy to get lost because you don't have points of reference and, suddenly, everything all around you looks the same. Take a compass if you have one; it might help you find the way back.

If you're going to explore near the sea, a lake, or a river, don't get too close to the water. There aren't crocodiles in many places . . . but a wave or a slippery stone could make you fall.

Also remember:

- Leave nests or burrows alone.

- Don't leave garbage on the ground or on riverbanks or in rivers.

- Don't pull up plants just for the sake of pulling them up.

Avoid lifting stones. There might be animals using them as a hiding place.

If you want to watch animals, try to stay silent so you don't scare them.

What to take with you

You certainly don't want to be cold, hungry, or uncomfortable when you go outside, so before you leave, make sure you have:

A hat and sunblock (Don't forget to apply sunblock regularly—in the countryside, you can get as much sun as you would during a day at the beach!)

A flashlight, in case you're out when it gets dark

Rain boots or shoes with rubber soles if you're going to watery places (such as rock pools)

Binoculars to see birds and other animals

A GPS or compass (Learn how to use them before you go!)

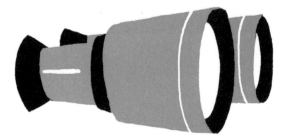

A notebook and pencil to write down and/or draw what you find

Comfortable boots (already broken in, of course)

A coat (Even if it's not chilly when you leave, the wind at the end of the day can become unpleasant.)

A flask, thermos, or bottle of water and a packed lunch

A guide to the countryside with helpful information, like names and details about animal and plant species, or types of rock—whichever are most appropriate for the places you're visiting. A guide to the stars would be great for a nighttime visit. You can take this book, too, of course!

LET`S SIT IN THE SHADE

TREES

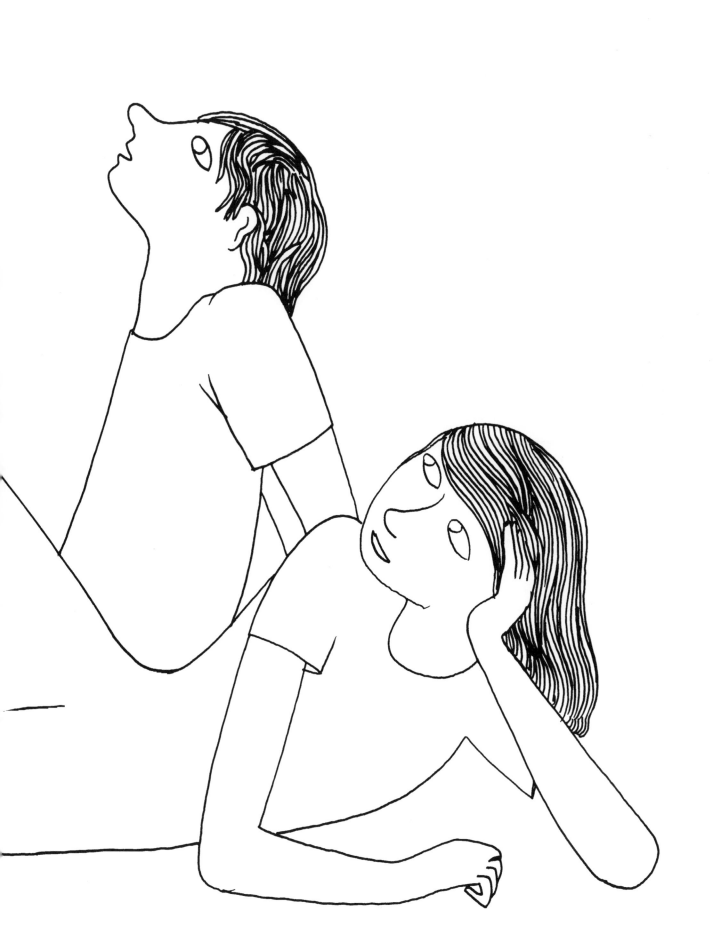

Lying under a tree on a hot day, we may just want to keep perfectly still, appreciating the peace and quiet of the shade.

If we look and listen carefully, though, we'll quickly discover that we're not alone: trees are the home and feeding place of lots of animals and sometimes a real playground where they hide, run, and climb.

You might get up from the shade and think, *Why don't I climb this tree, too?*

Crown: The crown, or the top part of the tree, is made up of branches and is where the leaves, flowers, and fruit are found.

Branches: The branches support the leaves and flowers.

Trunk: The trunk is the woody part that supports the weight of the tree.

Roots: The roots fix the tree to the ground. Roots work like a straw: the tree sucks food and water from the soil through them.

What is a tree?

A tree is a living being and belongs to the plant kingdom.

A tree has roots, a trunk, and a crown.

Compared to other plants, a tree can be very big!

And how does a tree grow so tall without falling down?

Trees have roots that grab on to the soil, and also a very strong trunk, which is able to support the weight of all the branches and leaves. (If the tree didn't have these, it would spread out low on the ground, like many other plants.)

What is the difference between a tree and a shrub?

A tree has a main stem (or trunk) and a crown with lots of branches, while in general, a shrub has several stems that grow from the ground. Normally, experts say that an adult tree is one that reaches at least 10 ft (3 m) in height.

- -

Speaking of height, did you know that the tallest tree in the world is a coast redwood, which can grow to be 380 ft (115 m) tall? That's the same as a 38-story building!

As well as being very tall, sequoias are considered to be the oldest living beings on the planet; some are more than 4,000 years old.

- -

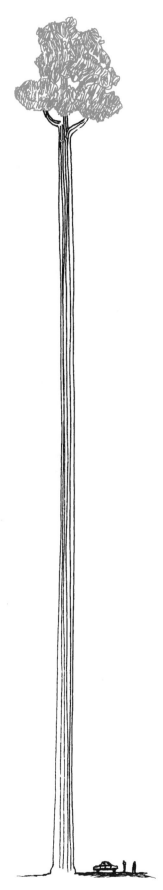

How do they grow?

Trees can grow in two ways: upward (in height) and outward (in width). This growth is accomplished by very active cells called meristematic cells. These cells are always multiplying and are able to make every kind of cell the tree needs: cells to make bark, flowers, and fruits.

What is there inside a trunk?

In a tree trunk, there is a very thin layer of cells called the cambium (2). The cambium is a factory that produces wood in two directions: inward, forming a layer called the xylem (1); and outward, building the phloem and the bark or the suber (cork tissue) (4).

With each year that goes by, the cambium makes new layers of these cells around the trunk, and the tree grows.

What are the xylem and phloem for?

A factory as tall as a tree can't function without elevators to move things up and down. The xylem and the phloem are these elevators:

- The xylem takes water with mineral salts (sap) from the roots to the leaves.
- The phloem sends the sap to all parts of the tree after it's been processed by the leaves.

What are those light and dark rings we see in a cut trunk?

They're the layers that are made as the tree grows. The lighter rings are formed during the spring and summer and are called the early wood; the darker rings are called the late wood because they're formed during the autumn and winter. In parts of the world where seasons aren't so defined, such as tropical climates, the growth rings aren't as easy to see.

What are roots for?

And why do trees push up the sidewalk?

All trees have roots, and all roots have the same functions: to secure trees to the ground, and to absorb water and other substances to feed the trees.

Some trees have roots that grow and grow, up to several yards deep. This is the case with eucalyptus trees, which, because they come from very dry places, find a way to get water wherever they are.

Other trees don't need to search so hard for water, and they have roots closer to the surface of the soil. This is the case with poplars as well as magnolia and ash trees. These are the ones that push up the sidewalk!

✳

Find fantastic trees in botanical gardens!

- -

In many cities, there are botanical gardens and centers you can visit. You can see a wide range of trees from all around the world!

Some examples of special roots

-- -- -- -- -- -- -- -- -- --

Most trees have subterranean roots, or roots that grow under the ground. But not all roots grow under the ground.

Aerial roots

Figs are examples of trees that can grow on walls or even on top of other trees. They are able to do this because they have aerial roots, which grow from their trunks until they reach the ground, where they find the water and nutrients they need.

Respiratory roots

Trees that live in places flooded with salt water, such as mangroves (a type of coastal forest in hot places like the tropics), also have to grow special roots. Because these roots grow in underwater soil, they aren't able to find the oxygen the trees need. To solve this problem, the trees developed pencil-like porous roots that grow up from the ground until they're above the water level, where the oxygen is. (Quite a trick!)

✻

**Lie on the ground
and look up at all the
leaves of the trees . . .**

. . . you'll see how good and
calm it makes you feel.

Learn to identify a tree

All trees have certain characteristics that define them, such as their height, their color, the shape of their crown, and the kind of leaf or fruit they have. All these aspects are useful for classifying and identifying the tree.

Let's start with the leaves

The first thing you can do to try to identify a tree is look at its leaves. By examining its leaves, you can see which large group of trees it belongs to: the conifers group or the broadleaf group.

For example, pines, firs, cypresses, and yews are conifers. You'll see that their leaves are like needles or overlap like scales. The leaves of these trees are almost always green, and they stay on the trees during the winter. Some of them, such as pines, produce resin, which protects them from insects or fungi.

Oaks and beeches belong to the broadleaf group. Both have wide leaves, and they drop their leaves in the coldest seasons.

When you hold a leaf in your hand, notice if it is wide or thin, hard or soft, and if it's winter, whether it's still green.

What conclusion do you make?

✳
Build a mobile in the shape of a tree

- - - - - - - - - - - - - -

Use dry twigs and nylon thread to create the frame. You can then hang a number of items from your "tree": leaves (real ones or ones you've drawn), or anything else you can find in a tree and you want to draw and cut out—butterflies, birds, squirrels, nests, flowers, or fruit.

- - - - - - - - - - - - - -

Why are leaves so different from one another?
Even though all leaves serve to capture light from the sun and carry out photosynthesis, the different types of leaves have adapted and have special characteristics according to the places where they first grew.

First of all, pines: because they had to adapt to cold, dry climates, they have leaves that are thin and hard, ones that are hardier and stop water from evaporating so quickly.

And trees from warmer forests, such as Judas trees, poplars, mulberries, or lindens, have wide leaves to enable them to transpire a lot of water.

Leaves: amazing sugar factories!

-- -- -- -- -- --

All living things need energy to live.

Animals eat plants or other animals to get energy; trees—and this might surprise you—get their energy from sugar! Sugar is produced in the leaves through photosynthesis. To make it, a tree needs water, mineral salts, carbon dioxide, and sunlight.

The best news for us humans is that when they make their sugar, trees give off oxygen, which we need to live!

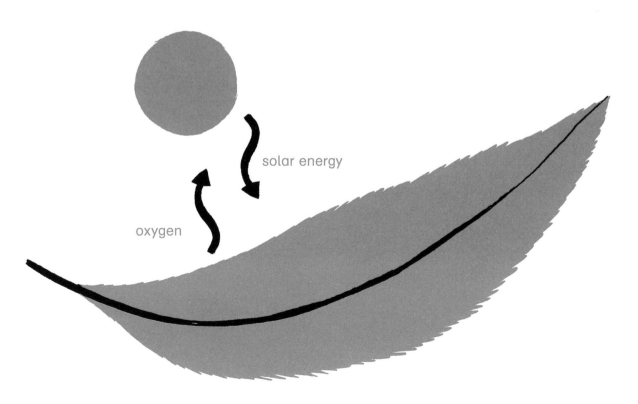

solar energy

oxygen

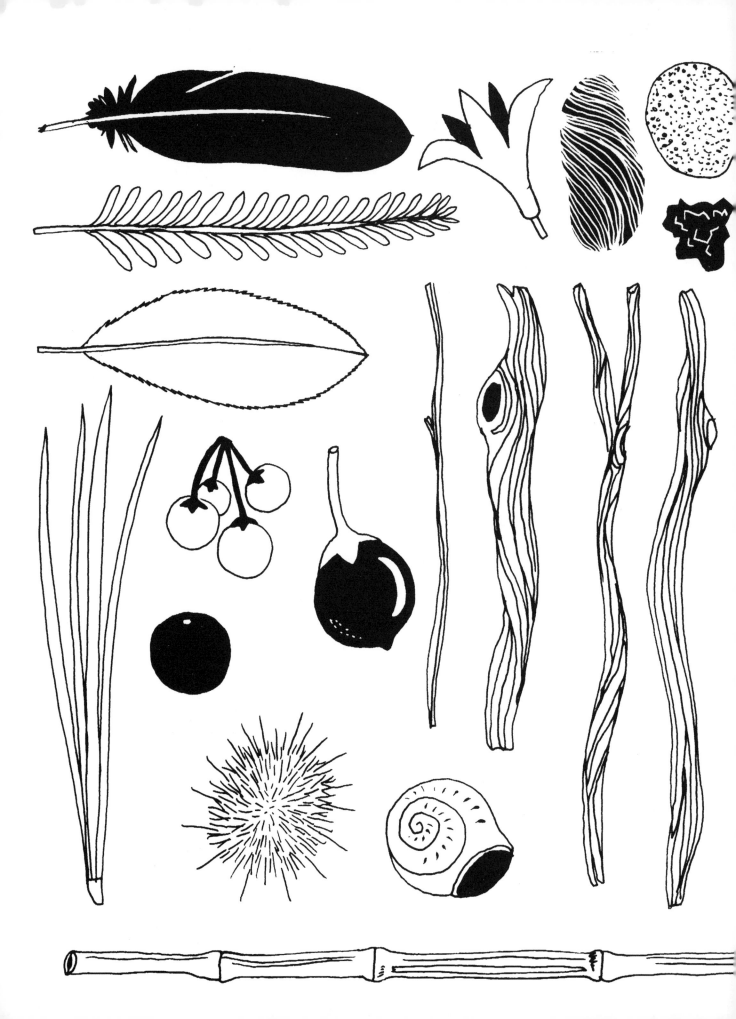

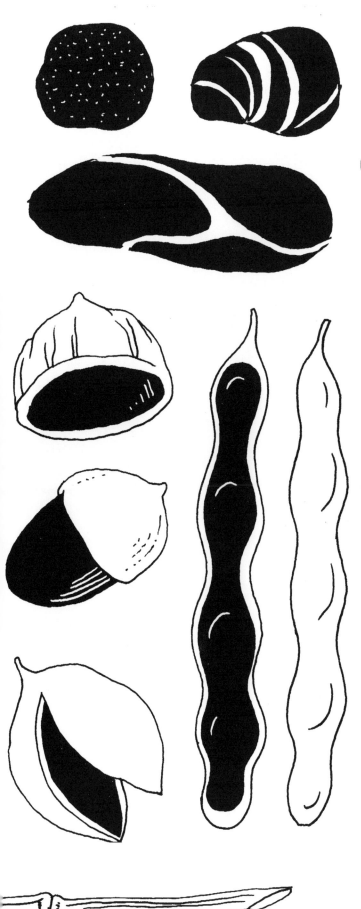

✳

Make sculpture inspired by Land Art, or Earth Art

- - - - - - - - - - - - - - - - - -

You can use sticks and other materials from nature, like leaves, stones, and soil. If you need inspiration, look for images by artists who use elements of nature in their work, such as Richard Long, Robert Smithson, Alberto Carneiro, Patrick Dougherty, and Mikael Hansen.

Why do some trees drop their leaves but others don't?
Tree leaves are sensitive and can freeze and die when it's cold for a long period of time—and if the leaves die, the tree dies. But trees have ways to solve this problem: some species drop their leaves on purpose when it's very cold and only grow new leaves when it's warm again. By doing so, they don't have to constantly replace the leaves that freeze from the cold and so save a lot of energy. Other species, like pines, invest in leaves that are better able to withstand low temperatures.

How do trees deal with the changes in the seasons?

Have you noticed that not all trees drop their leaves in the fall? And that on some trees the leaves turn red and on others they stay green?

When trees never lose their leaves, we say they're evergreen.
Of course, the leaves of these trees do fall, but only a few at a time and not during a certain season—new ones are always growing and we just don't notice. Examples are pines, laurels, Texas live oaks, and scrub oaks.

When trees lose their leaves in the fall, we say they're deciduous.
Red maple trees and English oaks are deciduous.

When trees keep their dry, reddish leaves in winter, we say their marcescent.
In this case, the leaves only fall when the new leaves begin to grow the following spring. An example is the northern red oak.

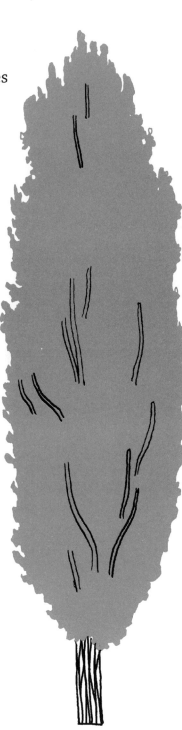

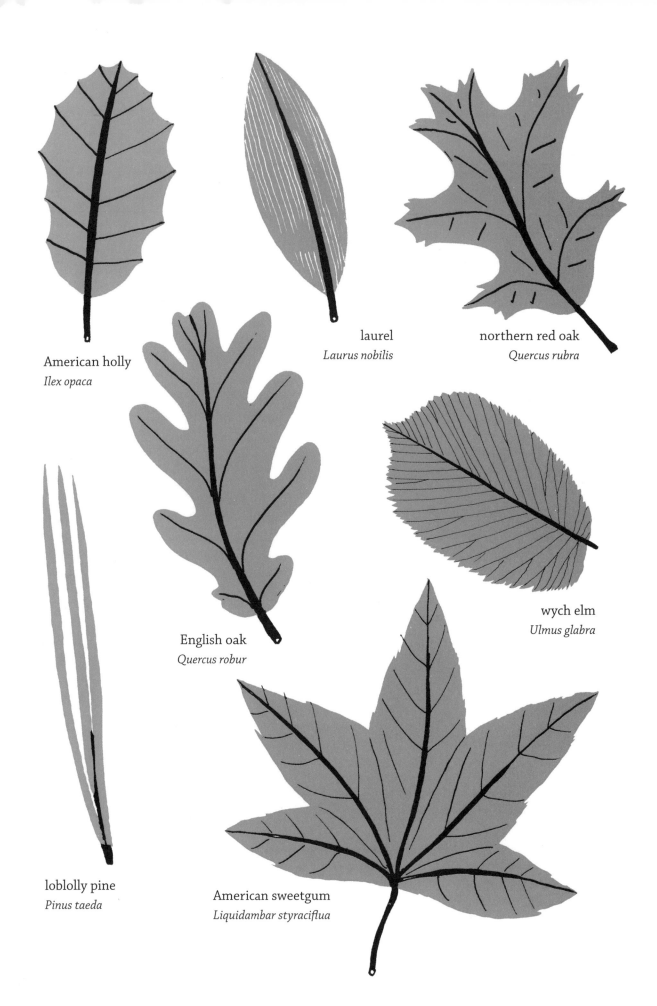

American holly
Ilex opaca

laurel
Laurus nobilis

northern red oak
Quercus rubra

English oak
Quercus robur

wych elm
Ulmus glabra

loblolly pine
Pinus taeda

American sweetgum
Liquidambar styraciflua

ginkgo
Ginkgo biloba

black poplar
Populus nigra

white willow
Salix alba

Pacific yew
Taxus brevifolia

black tupelo
Nyssa sylvatica

honey locust
Gleditsia triacanthos

yellow buckeye
Aesculus flava

Flowers, fruits, and seeds: do all trees have them?

All have seeds, but they're not always packaged in the same way.

Some trees have their seeds inside fleshy, tasty fruit—like pear, orange, or fig trees.

Others have their seeds inside harder fruits—like the walnut, almond, Texas live oak, and scrub oak.

And some trees have seeds that are stored inside fruits that aren't tasty for us humans but that other animals enjoy, such as the fruit of mastic trees, hawthorns, laurels, and many other trees. There are even trees that have seeds that aren't inside fruits, like the cones on pine and fir trees.

✳

An alphabet with twigs (and other items from nature)

- - - - - - - - - - - - - - - -

Look for letters in elements of nature: twigs, stones, patches of lichen and moss, or clouds. Try to find all the letters of the alphabet and make sure to take photos so you have a record of your nature alphabet—there are letters that will inevitably disappear for good.

- - - - - - - - - - - - - - - -

walnut leaves and fruit
Juglans regia

cork oak leaves and acorn
Quercus suber

almond leaves and
fruit
Prunus dulcis

ginkgo leaves and fruit
Ginkgo biloba

laurel leaves and fruit
Laurus nobilis

stone pinecone
Pinus pinea

hawthorn leaves and fruit
Crataegus monogyna

pear leaves and fruit
Pyrus communis

orange leaves, flower,
and fruit
Citrus sinensis

mastic tree
leaves and fruit
Pistacia lentiscus

Why do birds make their nests in trees?

Trees make extraordinary houses for many birds—and for other animals.

Because trees are so tall, many predators can't easily get to the animals' homes. Also, the leaves help to hide nests and protect them from the sun and rain. They also have another function: they're like the birds' "grocery store," where they can easily find lots of fruits and bugs to eat.

Is it a girl or a boy?

Did you know that trees can be male or female? And that sometimes they're both at once? It's true. When a species of tree has some trees that have male reproductive parts and others that have female parts, we say that the species is **dioecious** (like yew, white poplar, and ginkgo trees). When the male and female reproductive structures are on the same tree but different branches, we say that the species is **monoecious** (like cork oak and pine trees).

An important tree

The cork oak (*Quercus suber*) is a very special tree that grows in northwest Africa and southwest Europe—and especially in Spain and Portugal, which are the biggest producers of cork in the world.

What is cork?

Cork is the bark of the cork oak tree that's used to make stoppers for bottles, bags, insulation for houses, and many other things. But of course cork oaks don't make the cork just for us to put in bottles.

What is cork for in nature?

Cork oaks grow in places where the summer is hot and there are frequent fires. The main function of cork is to protect the tree, mainly from these fires. A fire can pass over a cork oak and burn all its leaves, but if it's got cork, the inside of the tree is protected and everything will grow again!

People learned how to take the cork from the trees without killing them, how to extract the cork so, little by little, it will grow back.

Why are there numbers painted on the trunks of cork oaks?

If you've ever seen a cork oak, you've probably seen a number painted on its bark.

This number is there so we know in which year the cork should be removed again. Cork isn't removed every year, only every nine or ten years.

There's a kind of code among cork producers: when they remove the cork, they paint the last numeral of the current year. For example, if the cork was removed in 2014, they paint a 4 on the tree; if it was removed in 2015, a 5, and so on. Because the cork should be removed every nine or ten years, then they know that, if the tree has a 4, the cork should be removed in 2023 or 2024. That way there are no mistakes!

❉
Visit a monumental tree!

- -

Monumental trees are trees that distinguish themselves from others of the same species by their size, shape, age, rarity, or historical interest.

These trees are considered of the public interest and are treated like national monuments. Investigate where you can find some of the most important ones in your area.

Did you know that cork has even been to space?

-- -- -- -- -- --

For many years, cork has been used on NASA's trips to space. This is because it is fire resistant and an excellent insulator. In fact, if you line a whole room with cork, no one outside the room will hear what's going on in there.

· - - - - - - - - - - - - -

✳

Build a swing and reach the clouds

- -

Here are some tips for your
safety and for the health of
the tree:

- Choose trees with harder
  wood (e.g., English oaks,
  beech trees, or maple).

- Choose branches that
  are about 20 ft (6 m) off
  the ground, measure
  more than 8 in (20 cm)
  in diameter, and are
  wide enough that they
  don't bend when the
  swing is attached.

- The swing should be about
  3–5 ft (1–1.5 m) away from
  the main trunk.

- The branch has to be
  healthy. Avoid branches
  that have any signs of
  disease, infestation, or
  cracks, or that have narrow
  attachments to the main
  branch. Never use a dead
  branch—it might break!

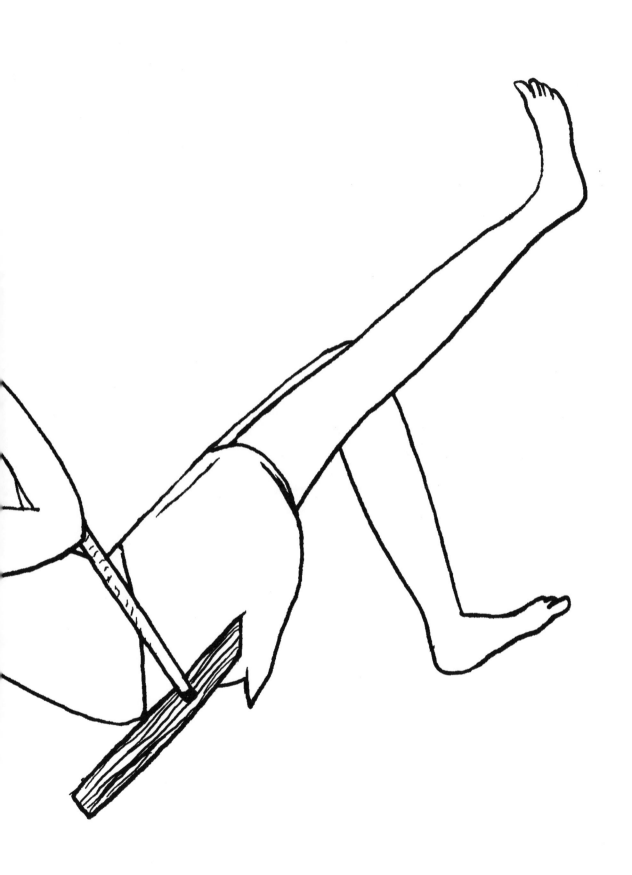

Does everything in nature serve a purpose?

Flowers could simply be pretty things for us to look at . . . but in reality, flowers aren't just attractive parts of plants: they play a very important role in the life of the plant.

What could that role be?

Get ready for a world of colors, smells, and buzzing sounds . . .

Where are they?

Everyone knows about colorful flowers like
roses, carnations, tulips, lilies, and marigolds.
But not all flowers are as big and brightly
colored.
Some are so small and inconspicuous that
we can only see them with the help of a
magnifying glass. There are others that
grow without anyone having planted
them—we find them in meadows,
vegetable gardens, or even in cracks
in the sidewalk . . .

In gardens and yards, there are some
flowers that aren't native to the area—
they have been planted in places around
the world simply because they're beautiful,
for instance, roses, pansies, hibiscus,
and dahlias.

In vegetable gardens, you can find squash,
watermelon, melon, and cucumber flowers.
And also onion, carrot, or passion fruit flowers
(which are hermaphrodites and have the
reproductive organs of both sexes).

Flowers can appear in some unexpected places.
If you're in a town or city, you might see small

dahlia

plants growing in cracks in the sidewalk—we usually call these plants weeds. These plants also have flowers.

On the <u>walls or roofs of buildings</u>, there can even be flowers, such as white stonecrop, navelwort, and Kenilworth ivy.

On <u>pavements and paths</u>, you might see clover, prickly sow thistle, field mustard, or blue pimpernel.

Where there is a <u>bit more soil</u>, you might see Bermuda buttercup, milk thistle, dandelions, Cornish mallow, musk storksbill, daisies, or poppies.

In <u>the countryside</u>, you can see bushes that have flowers, like species of rockrose, heather, rosemary, or French lavender.

Environmentally-friendly sidewalks?

You might think the spaces and cracks in sidewalk are small. But if we added up all the soil in these spaces, we'd have a really big area! Many plants and critters live here. Also, this soil is important because it lets water through—otherwise the water wouldn't filter back into the ground.

Pansy
Viola x wittrockiana

Hibiscus
Hibiscus rosa-sinensis

Pumpkin flower
Cucurbita pepo

Onion flower
Allium cepa

French lavender
Lavandula stoechas

Passion fruit flower
Passiflora edulis

Watermelon flower
Citrullus lanatus

Kenilworth ivy
Cymbalaria muralis

Carrot flower
Daucus carota

Muskmelon flower
Cucumis melo

Cucumber flower
Cucumis sativus

White clover
Trifolium repens

Heather
Calluna vulgaris

Prickly sow thistle
Sonchus asper

Rosemary
Rosmarinus officinalis

Hawkbit
Leontodon taraxacoides

What are flowers for?

Flowers exist so plants can reproduce—in other words, they exist so new plants can grow.

How did flowers appear in the world?
Flowers are made from modified leaves. Millions of years ago, when there weren't yet flowers, some plants started to very slowly change their leaves, until they transformed into the flowers we know today.

Why do flowers smell so good?
People normally really like the smell of flowers. But it's not *us* the flowers want to attract with their lovely smell: flowers are designed to attract animals, normally insects, that can take their pollen to another flower of the same species and pollinate it.

What is pollination?
Pollination is the transfer of pollen from the stamen to the gynoecium. This meeting generates the seeds—the baby plants.

When pollination takes place inside of a flower or between two flowers of the same plant, it is called self-pollination. When it happens between flowers of different plants, it is called cross-pollination, which is more common. In cross-pollination, the plants need help (usually from insects or the wind) to reproduce, and to get this help, they use certain tricks . . .

✳

Identify the parts of a flower

- - - - - - - - - - - - - -

Identifying the parts of a flower isn't easy because some flowers are close together on the same base, and so the different parts are very small and/or difficult to identify.

Tips:
- Collect flowers from various plants, preferably big ones, because they're easier to identify.

- Carefully separate the various parts of flowers and try to identify them according to the diagram on the next page.

- You'll see that flowers can be very different depending on species, but it's most common to have several stamens and colored petals and for the gynoecium to have one pistil.

- - - - - - - - - - - - - -

Corolla
The corolla is the name for all the petals together.

Gynoecium
The gynoecium is the female part of the flower. It's formed by carpels, which produce the ovules.

Androecium
The androecium is the male part of the flower. It's formed by the stamens, which produce the pollen.

Petals
The petals are the colored parts that attract insects.

Calyx
The calyx is the name for the sepals, the small green parts that protect the flower when it's still a bud.

What's the main trick for attracting insects?

It's a sweet trick . . . Some insects, such as bees, feed off nectar, the sugary liquid that flowers produce in addition to pollen. While the bees are collecting the nectar, the pollen sticks to their legs, and when the bees fly away and land on other flowers, they leave the pollen behind—and pollen is needed for fertilization.

Some flowers smell quite pleasant, but some produce horrible smells, like the smell of rotting meat. Instead of pretty butterflies, these flowers are attempting to attract flies, insects that love stinky things!

✳ Make a crown of flowers

- -

You can make a crown of flowers by twisting together daisies. Gather several with long stems of about the same length. Take two flowers, cross the stems, and twist them together. Add more flowers, in a circlular shape, until you make a crown the size of your head.

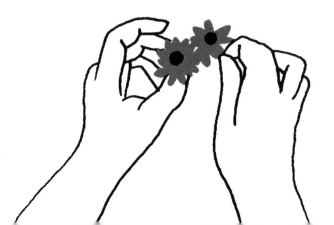

Not everything is as it seems

(other tricks plants use to attract insects)

- -

Flowers that imitate insects

There are flowers that don't just have colorful petals to attract pollinators. Some, like orchids, have transformed their petals and sepals so they look like insects. There are some orchids that look like a particular species of insect, and only that species can pollinate them.

Flowers with runways

To guarantee that animals find the pollen and nectar, some flowers have a kind of line drawn on them to show the way. These lines aren't always visible to us, but for the insects, which have a different kind of vision than we do, these lines really stand out.

orchid

tulip

Petals that aren't petals

Some flowers have "almost" petals—these flowers have found a way to imitate a pretty corolla by making their sepals very large and colorful so they look like petals. This is the case with tulips and lilies. There are plants that go even further, having leaves as colorful as a large flower. The bougainvillea is an example of this. Try looking inside this "false flower," and there you'll find the real (and very tiny) white flowers, tucked inside the colorful leaves.

And after the flower?

Flowers turn into fruits, which are able to protect the seeds and also attract animals by how they look, smell, and taste. Why is this so important?

Because it's quite likely that a seed hidden inside of a tasty fruit will be eaten by an animal. And later, when it's time for that animal to poop, it's also likely that the animal will be far away from the plant where it picked the fruit . . . And so the plant meets its goal: to spread its seeds without its offspring growing too close to it and competing for the same resources (soil, light, water, and nutrients).

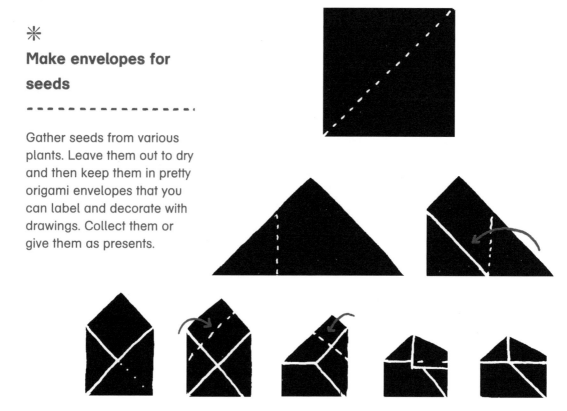

✳

Make envelopes for seeds

- - - - - - - - - - - - - - - - -

Gather seeds from various plants. Leave them out to dry and then keep them in pretty origami envelopes that you can label and decorate with drawings. Collect them or give them as presents.

Take a close look at a daisy

Look at a daisy, with a magnifying glass if you can.

How many flowers do you see? Just one? Really?
If you look closely, the middle part is made of lots of tiny flowers—so many you can't even count them! The outside has larger petals and gives us the impression that we're looking at a single flower with a large yellow "eye."

<u>Really, what we looking at isn't a flower. It's an inflorescence—a lot of flowers grouped together.</u>

There are other "flowers" that have this feature: marigolds, dahlias, chrysanthemums, and gerberas. These all have a kind of inflorescence (called a capitulum) and belong to a large family called composite flowers.

These flowers don't have to do as much work because only the ones on the outside have to spend energy making big petals to attract pollinators. But in the end, they all benefit.

● **Make a poppy dancer**

- -

You can make a delicate dancer by bending the petals of a poppy down toward its stem and tying them with a bit of grass or a thin stem to make the "waist."

Then push a stick up through the part that will be the dancer's body. You can move the stick to make your poppy dance.

Note: The hardest part is to turn the petals downward without tearing them off—the petals are very fragile.

✳ ✳

Make a bouquet of wildflowers

Have fun combining colors, shapes, and sizes to make a pretty bouquet. You can tie it with any natural material that will work as a ribbon. **Then give someone your bouquet!**

- - - - - - - - - - - -

Stop and smell the roses (and all the other flowers!)

When you walk through the countryside or a garden, close your eyes and try to notice the different smells in the air. Can you identify any of them?

TO THE
CENTER OF
THE
EARTH

ROCKS

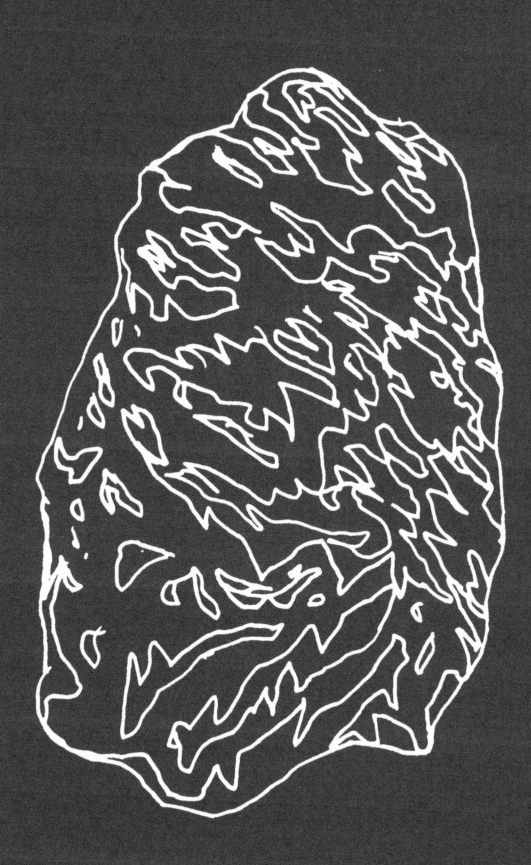

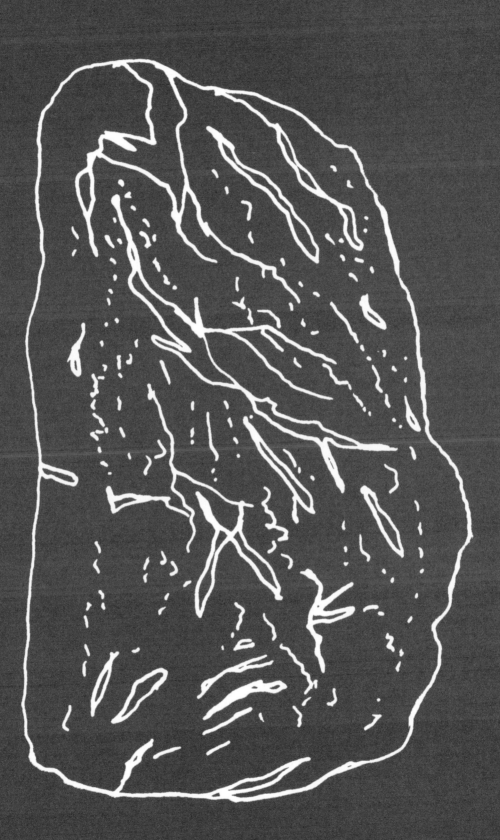

When you're out for a walk, think about this: under your feet, down at the center of the earth, are giant chunks of rock that are millions of years old!

Silent, strong, and mysterious, nature is always there.

Planet Earth or planet Rock?

People say that planet Earth could be called planet Water because it has a lot of water on its surface, but it wouldn't be wrong to call it planet Rock because it's mostly made of rock. Rocks are formed of minerals that combine in different ways, which creates rocks with different properties.

On Earth's surface, the rocks are in a solid state. But down in the planet's core, there's molten rock bubbling away . . .

Blop, blop, blop!

What are rocks?

The rocks you see all around—on the beach, in rivers, on mountains—are mixtures of minerals joined together to make a solid.

Cement and bricks aren't rocks: they're—very impressive!—man-made creations.

Examples of rocks include granite, limestone, basalt, marble, schist, and sandstone.

- -

If Earth was an egg, its crust (on the surface) would be the shell. This shell is covered with water, ice, soil, sand, vegetation, animal and plant remains, etc. Dig down a bit, and soon enough we hit the rock that covers the whole planet.

Mineral + mineral = rock?

Almost all rocks are formed of two or more minerals. For example, granite is a combination of the minerals quartz and feldspar. (It also contains mica but in a smaller amount.) But it's not enough to put two or three minerals together to make a rock . . .

A rock recipe: You have the ingredients (in this case, the minerals), and you'll use these to make a cake (the rock). To make a particular kind of cake, you have to have the ingredients in the right amounts. Then you have to mix and beat the ingredients and heat or cool them, transforming them or cooking them at a precise temperature. The same thing happens with rocks.

And finally, what are minerals?

There are over 4,000 minerals on Earth, all made from chemical elements (oxygen, carbon, etc.) combined in different ways. Quartz, for example, the most abundant mineral on the planet, is formed of two chemical elements: silica and oxygen.

So what are stones?

What we call stones or pebbles are smaller pieces of rock that have broken off from the "bedrock." A lot of the time, as with larger rocks, these smaller stones change shape and texture through weathering and erosion (by water, wind, or temperature, for example) and can become round and smooth, like some you'll find by the ocean or a river.

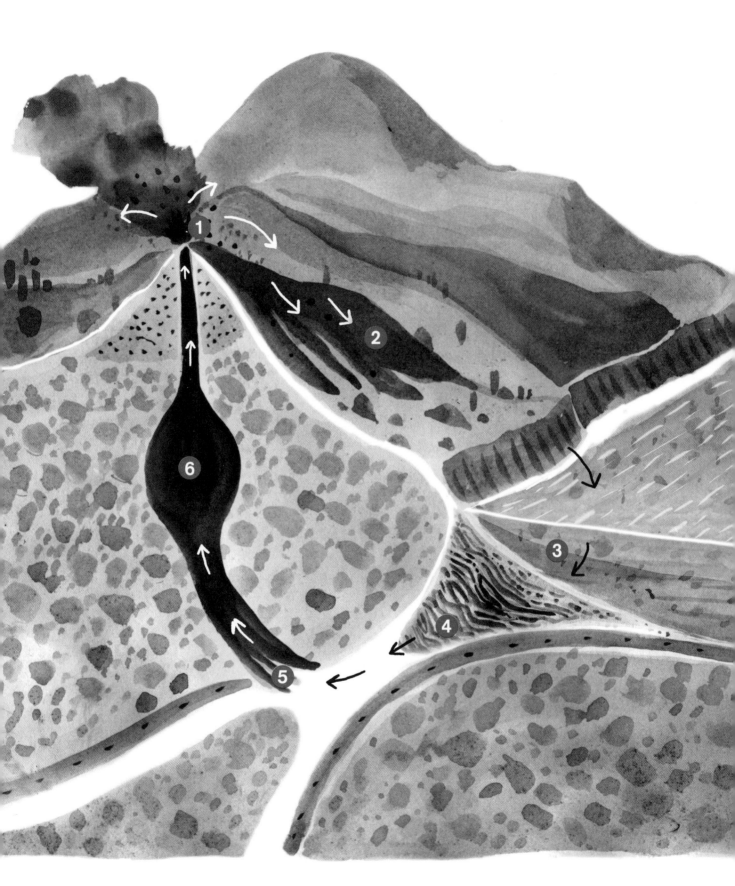

Nature: a great big rock-recycling machine

The materials that make up rocks are never "lost"—they're always changing and being transformed (just like water in the water cycle).

With rocks, this cycle can take thousands or even millions of years.

The movements of the earth (caused by different pressures and temperatures) push solid or liquid magma to the surface and create <u>igneous rocks</u> **(1)**.

(2) <u>On the surface</u>, some of these rocks are split into pieces by weathering and erosion, from variations in temperature and water, wind, etc.

Some of these sediments are transported, deposited, compacted, and consolidated (whew!) creating <u>sedimentary rocks</u> **(3)**.

The movements of the earth keep on going, pressing and heating these rocks, forming <u>metamorphic rocks</u> **(4)**.

Some rocks return to the <u>earth's interior</u> **(5)**. When they melt again, they form <u>magma</u> **(6)** once more . . .

And a new cycle begins.

What kind of rock are paving stones?

Some countries, like Brazil and Portugal, are famous for their patterned sidewalks with designs and pictures in black and white. This traditional style of paving is called a Portuguese pavement, and it is usually made with blocks of limestone (for the white stones) and basalt (for the black stones). Depending on the region and the availability of geological resources, paving stones can vary. In some areas, paving stones are blocks of granite.

Rock hard! (Are there minerals in my body, too?)

Of course. You know by now that in nature things are always moving and influencing one another. The same thing happens with the minerals that make up rocks: minerals get into underground water (aquifers), surface water (like rivers, streams, and lakes), and seawater, as well as soil, where trees, vegetables, and fruits grow. When we eat and drink, our bodies, which are also part of nature and part of this chain, receive the minerals we need to live. We couldn't live without rocks and minerals!

What is the hardest rock out there?

There is a scale that measures the hardness of minerals. It's called the Mohs scale of mineral hardness, and it measures how easily a mineral is scratched by another. From the softest to the hardest:

- talc (easily scratched by a fingernail)
- gypsum (can be scratched by a fingernail)
- calcite (can be scratched by a copper coin)
- fluorite (can be scratched by an iron nail)
- apatite (can be scratched by glass)
- feldspar (can be scratched by a penknife)
- quartz (can be scratched by a steel blade)
- topaz (can be scratched by a file)
- corundum
- diamond

The hardness of a rock depends on the level of hardness of the minerals it's made from. With this scale, now you know that the champion of hardness is the diamond!

Is there rock that can float?

- - - - - - - - - - - - - - - - -

Yes, but only one. Pumice stone is a volcanic rock formed when molten lava (which is rich in gases) is projected into the atmosphere and cools, forming a rock that looks more like a sponge because it has lots of holes. It's the only stone that floats because it's a lot less dense than water. Get a pumice stone (you can easily buy these) and do experiments in water.

- - - - - - - - - - - - - - - - -

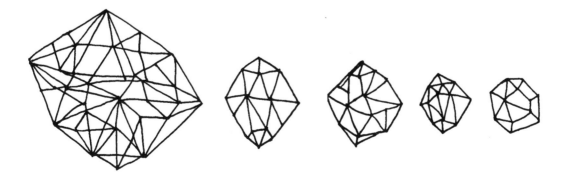

What is this stone I found?

- - - - - - - - - - - - - - - - - -

That depends on the area where you found it! And it also depends on the characteristics of that stone. To discover which family of rocks it belongs to, you have to look at your stone closely and find the answers to some questions:

- What color is it?
- Is it made from grains of different colors?
- Can you see any large crystals?
- Is it smooth or rough?
- Is it shiny?
- Is it very hard or does it crumble?
- Does it easily split into layers?
- Is it permeable or impermeable?
- Does it float?

By looking at the next pages, you might be able to come to some conclusions about your stone.

- - - - - - - - - - - - - - - - - -

Properties of some rocks

Limestone
- Light colors
- Hard
- Dense texture
- Variable permeability
- Doesn't crumble, but splits easily
- Reacts with acid

Granite
- Speckled, various colors
- Hard
- Grainy texture
- Low permeability
- Doesn't crumble or split easily

Clay
- Brown, yellow, green colors
- Can be molded when wet
- Cracks when dry
- Fine-grained texture
- Impermeable
- Crumbles easily

Schist
- Dark colors (gray, brown)
- Not very hard
- Layered texture
- Variable permeability
- Splinters easily

Basalt
- Dark colors (black)
- Very hard
- Very fine grains
- Low permeability
- Doesn't break easily

Marble
- Variable colors (white, gray, pink, etc.)
- Very hard
- Smooth texture
- Impermeable
- Doesn't crumble or split easily
- Reacts with acid

Note: Do not experiment with rocks and chemicals unless a responsible adult is supervising!

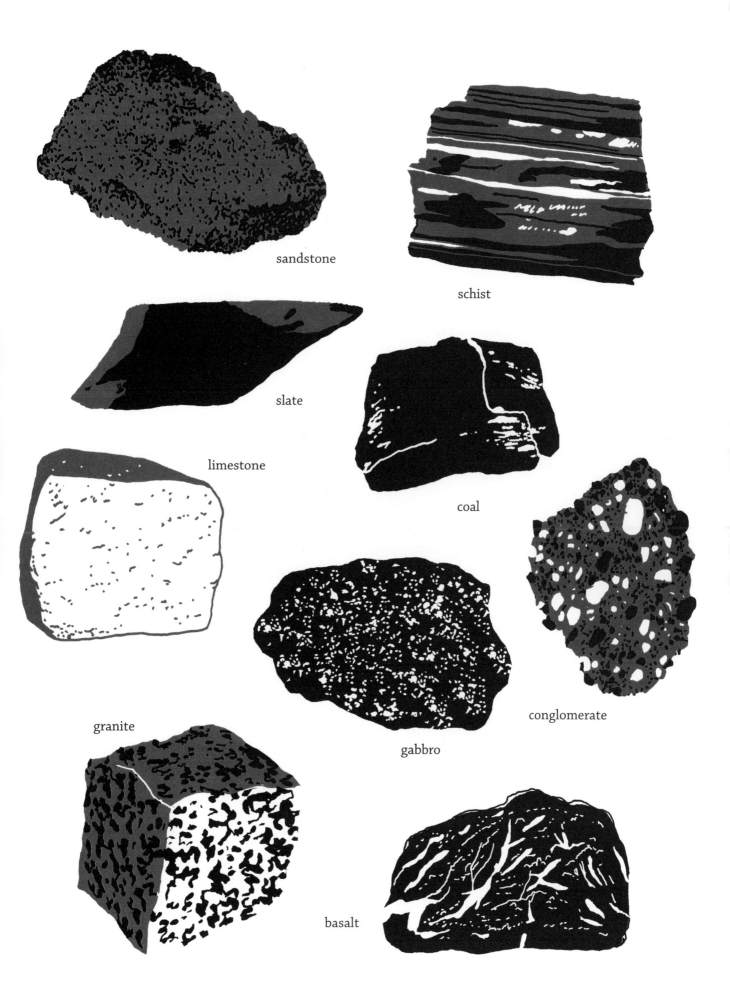

sandstone

schist

slate

limestone

coal

granite

conglomerate

gabbro

basalt

Do rocks move?

We're used to thinking of rocks as immobile, stable things. Is this right?

In actual fact rocks do move all on their own—especially the ones that form our planet's crust. They move so slowly and gradually that we hardly ever notice, except when these movements are bigger and cause earthquakes or tremors. But even most earthquakes are so weak that people don't feel them, they're only picked up by seismographs (machines used by scientists to detect movements in the ground).

Do continents move too?

If the rocks that form our planet's crust are moving, that means the continents move too. Approximately 175 million years ago, there was just a single supercontinent, called Pangea, surrounded by a single ocean, Panthalassa. This supercontinent started to separate into smaller continents, which kept moving very slowly, until they arrived in the

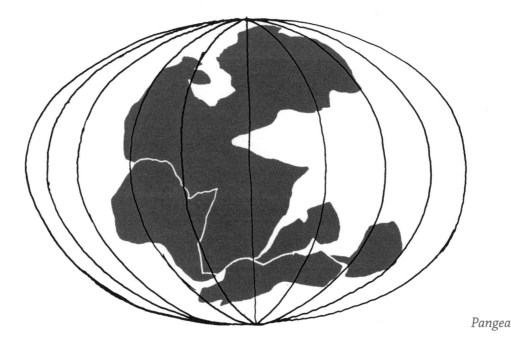

Pangea

positions we know today. And the continents are still moving now. For example, America and Eurasia are moving away from one another: they move about $^3/_4$ in (2 cm) per year in opposite directions—which means that the Atlantic Ocean is getting wider, and the Pacific Ocean is getting narrower.

How do we know that the continents moved (and are still moving)?

Today there are GPS machines (which work in the same way as the GPS in a car) that measure the speed that continents are moving. But for a long time the strongest evidence for <u>continental drift</u> (this is the name for the movement of the large plates of rock that form Earth's crust) were . . . animals!

When scientists studied the fossils of animals that lived on Earth many millions of years ago, they found very similar species on continents that today are separated by wide oceans. The most probable explanation is that these continents were together when these animals walked upon them.

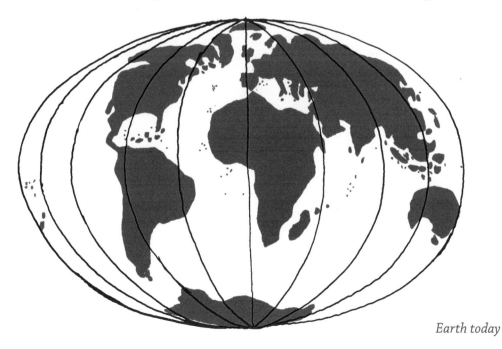

Earth today

Water dripping day by day wears the hardest rocks away

Even the hardest rocks can't withstand the effect of wind and water passing over them constantly. Over many years, the rocks break apart into small (minuscule) pieces, which are moved to other places. The sand on beaches, for example, is made up of these particles (sometimes mixed with the remains of mollusk shells). This phenomenon of wearing away rock by the elements is called <u>erosion</u>.

The water in rivers and the ocean is one of the main causes of rock erosion. This is why at mouths of rivers we sometimes find large areas of mud: these are sediments carried by rivers along their course that get deposited when the speed of the river decreases as it meets the sea.

One of the most visible forms of erosion caused by water can be seen on sea cliffs. The effect of waves and tides, as well as the wind that blows off the sea, wears the rocks away, forming cliffs and sometimes caves. Larger or smaller pieces fall to the beach and end up getting eroded as well.

Another piece of evidence for erosion by water are river valleys. Notice how the shape of a valley is different according to the part of the river. In the areas farthest upstream (nearest to the source), where the river flows faster, valleys are usually narrower and deeper, while in the areas closer to the river's mouth, where the river flows more slowly, valleys are flatter and more open.

The land around the lowest areas of rivers is generally very rich because of all the sediments carried by the water. This makes these areas excellent for agriculture. It was precisely in these areas that the first human civilizations established themselves. Even today we can see that many big cities are near or on the mouths of big rivers.

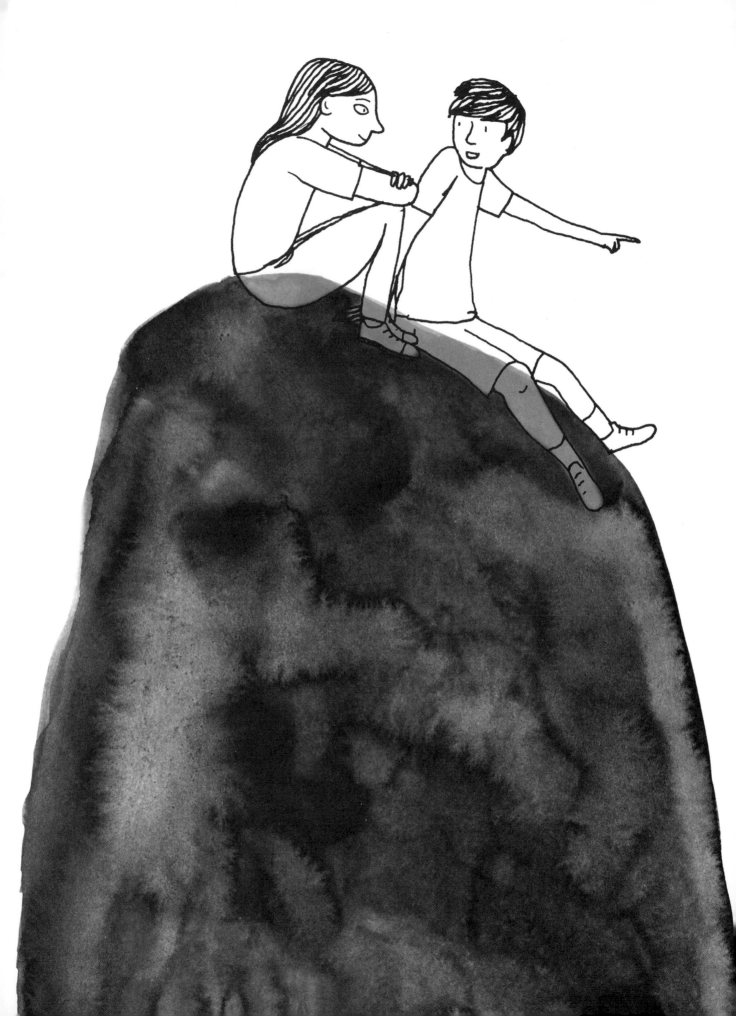

● ● ● ● ●

Collect the many textures of rocks

- - - - - - - - - - - - - - - -

Use bits of mud or modeling paste to collect the textures of rocks. Press rocks firmly into the soft material, which will mold around the rocks. Look at all the differences!

- - - - - -

Draw with schist

- - - - - - - - - - - - - - - -

If you happen to walk through an area with lots of schist, look carefully for any (natural) walls of clayish schist where the layers of rock are coming loose. Take a piece and try scratching a flat piece of schist. You'll see how schist can be very soft and will crumble, like chalk, as you write and draw with it.

- - - - - -

Touch rocks with your eyes closed

- - - - - - - - - - - - - - - -

You can feel the texture of rocks better if you close your eyes. Notice that there are smooth stones (like marble) and others that are very rough (like granite), some that have layers (like schist), some that are very cold, others that are warmer, and some that even have a smell (argillite).

- - - - - -

How many different stones . . .

- - - - - - - - - - - - - - - -

. . . can you find when you're out for a walk? How about near the ocean? Or on a riverbank?
Make a collection and create an exhibit. Organize a route for visitors and write small labels with whatever information you like. (But don't move big stones from where they are—there might be animals living underneath!)

- - - - - -

A world of grains in the palm of your hand

- - - - - - - - - - - - - - - -

Sand is made from grains that come from the disintegration of rocks caused by erosion. If you look at a handful of sand, you might see that the grains are all the same—in this case, the sand must be made from a single type of rock. But it's possible that you have lots of different colored grains in your hand—in this case, each grain comes from a different kind of rock. You could be holding bits of the whole world in your hand!

- - - - - -

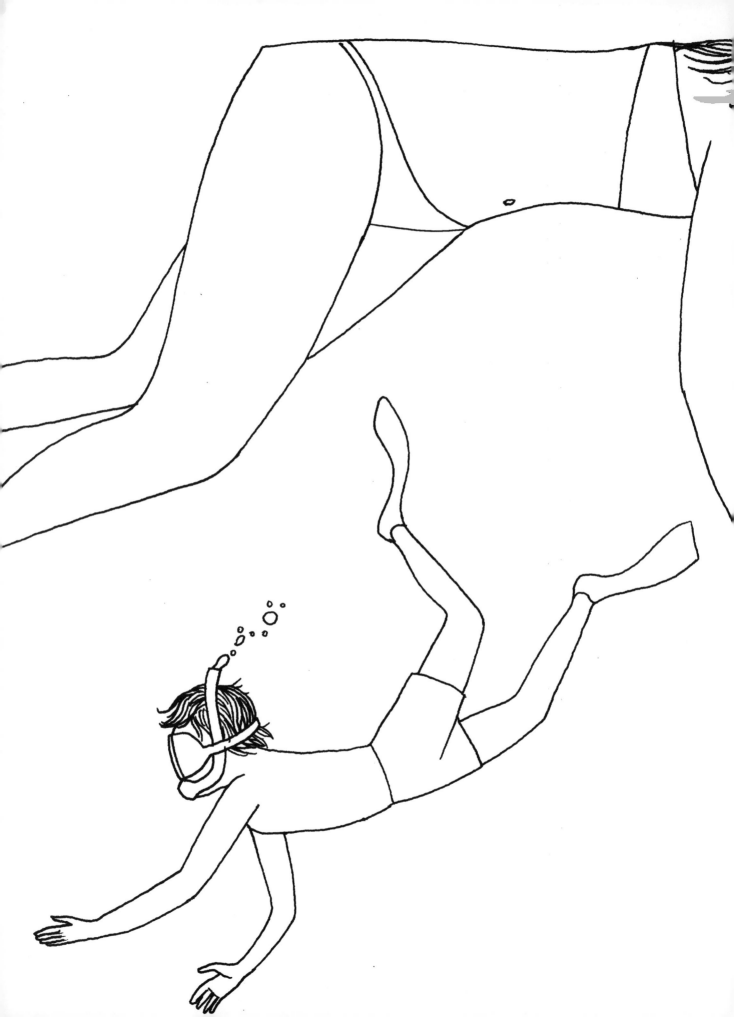

HOW ABOUT WE GO TO THE BEACH?

OCEANS, BEACHES, AND TIDE POOLS

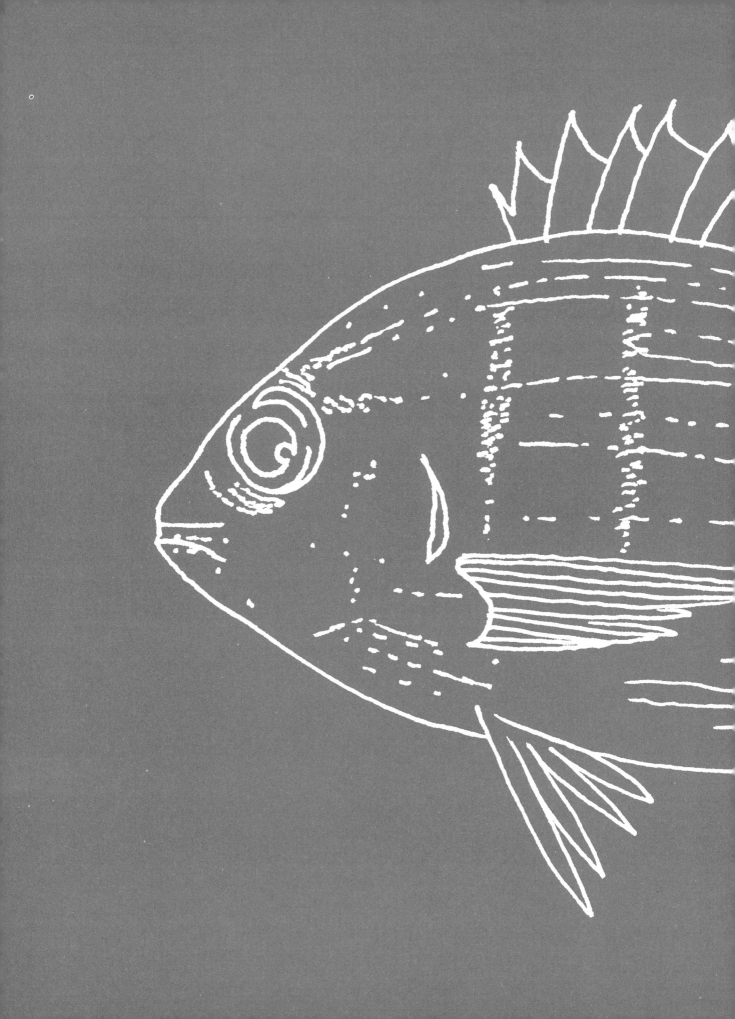

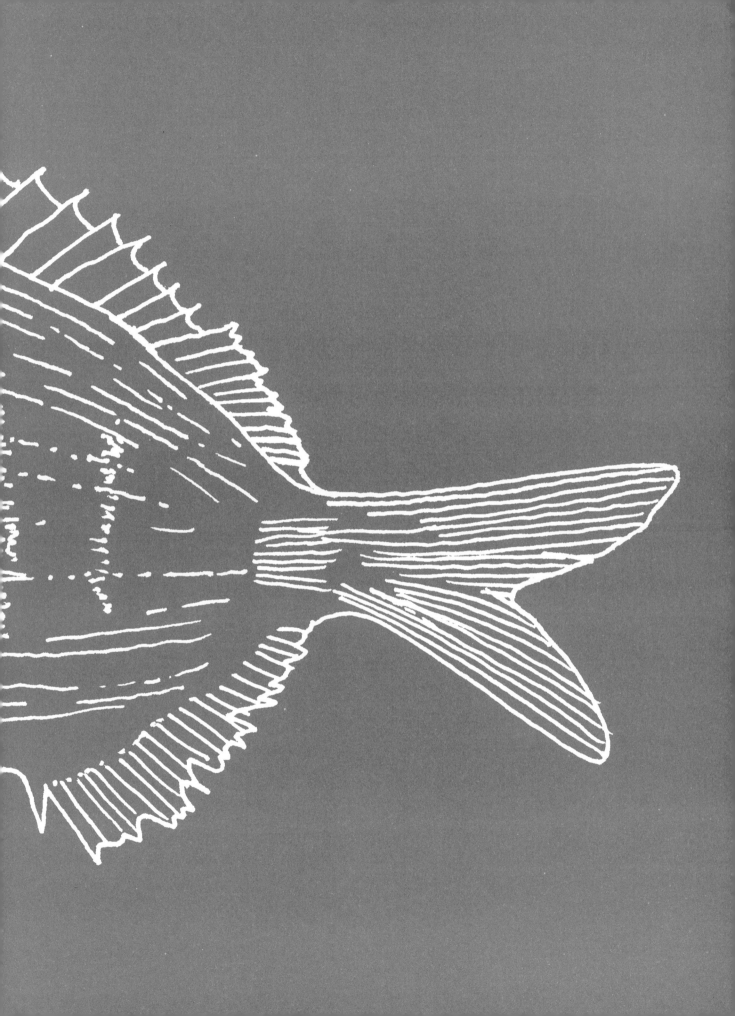

The beach is a very special place, not only because it reminds us of summer vacations, but also because there—with our feet in the sand and the waves arriving every second—we can feel nature in all its force.

Why don't you take your shoes off and come to the beach? There's a lot here to see and learn.

Take a dip with us!

If the water that comes from rivers is freshwater, and rivers flow into the ocean . . . where does the salt in the ocean come from?

As rivers flow over rocks, the minerals that the rocks are made of gradually dissolve in the water. It's these minerals that make salt.

Over the course of millions of years, these small amounts of salt have been carried to the ocean and have accumulated there . . . up to the point that when you get a mouthful of seawater today, there's only one taste it can have: it's very salty!

And why is the ocean blue?

If you look at seawater closely, it's transparent, like the water that comes out of a faucet. So why does it look blue when we see it from a distance?

Some people say it's because the ocean reflects the blue of the sky, which isn't true. The ocean is blue because it mainly reflects blue light, but this effect is only noticeable when there's a large amount of water (especially where the ocean is the deepest).

The different shades of blue that we see are caused by the shadows of clouds, the colors of the seafloor, or by sediments.

Why isn't the beach always the same width?

At many beaches, the ocean is sometimes really far away and we have to walk a long distance to take a dip. This happens because of the tide: when the tide is in, the water comes farther up the beach; when the tide is out, the water stays further away.

Why are there tides?

The sun and moon exert an invisible force on Earth called gravity. However, the moon is closer to us, so it is mostly responsible for tides, pulling the seawater as our planet spins. And this is why when the tide is in at your beach, it is out at the beach on the other side of the ocean.

How do tides work?

Tides work in cycles: as soon as the tide is completely in, it immediately starts to go out again; in a little over six hours, it will be out. Then it starts to come in again, and after another six hours or so, it's in once more.

Spring tides and neap tides

The sun also exerts a gravitational force on Earth, but because it's much farther away, this force isn't as strong as that of the moon. It's still perceptible, though. What happens?

When the sun and moon are aligned (which happens at the full moon and the new moon), the two forces pull in the same direction and the water moves more: these are "spring tides." Then during the first and third quarters of the moon, the sun and moon are not aligned, and they each pull a different direction. (The moon pulls harder because it's closer.) These tides are less strong: they're "neap tides."

The tides are also not the same throughout the year: close to the equinoxes (in March and September) are the strongest spring tides of the year; close to the solstices (in December and June) are the weakest neap tides.

A dictionary for waves

In the world of waves, it's again important that everything has a name and that these names mean the same for everyone.

When you hear someone mention the <u>waterline</u> **(1)**, you know that it's the line that separates the surface of the water from the depths below; the lowest part is called the <u>trough</u> **(2)**; the highest part is the <u>crest</u> **(3)**. The distance between the trough and the crest is called the <u>wave height</u> **(4)**; the distance between two crests or between two troughs is the <u>wavelength</u> **(5)**.

How are waves formed?

The wind blows on the ocean and starts to make very small waves, which make the ocean "rippled." These "ripples"(6) increase the exposed surface of the ocean, which means that more of the wind's energy transfers to the water. The waves gradually gain energy, strength, and height.

When the wind blows in a certain place, the waves that form there start off all jumbled. Then, as the waves leave that area, they become gradually more regular. When we see them arrive at the coast all lined up—the swell (7) that surfers like so much— the waves have traveled several miles.

6

3

5

4

2

How do tide pools form?

As the tide goes out, it exposes sand and rocks that minutes before were underneath the water. We call this exposed area <u>intertidal</u>. When this area is rocky, the seawater gets trapped in small holes, forming tide pools.

So do animals get trapped in there?
Yes, especially the animals that are stuck to rocks and aren't able to move a lot on their own, like mussels, limpets, anemones, and sea urchins, as well as any that aren't very skilled at walking on land, like fish and shrimp. There are others that like moving from tide pool to tide pool, risking being seen by whoever is passing by—this is the case with crabs and octopuses.

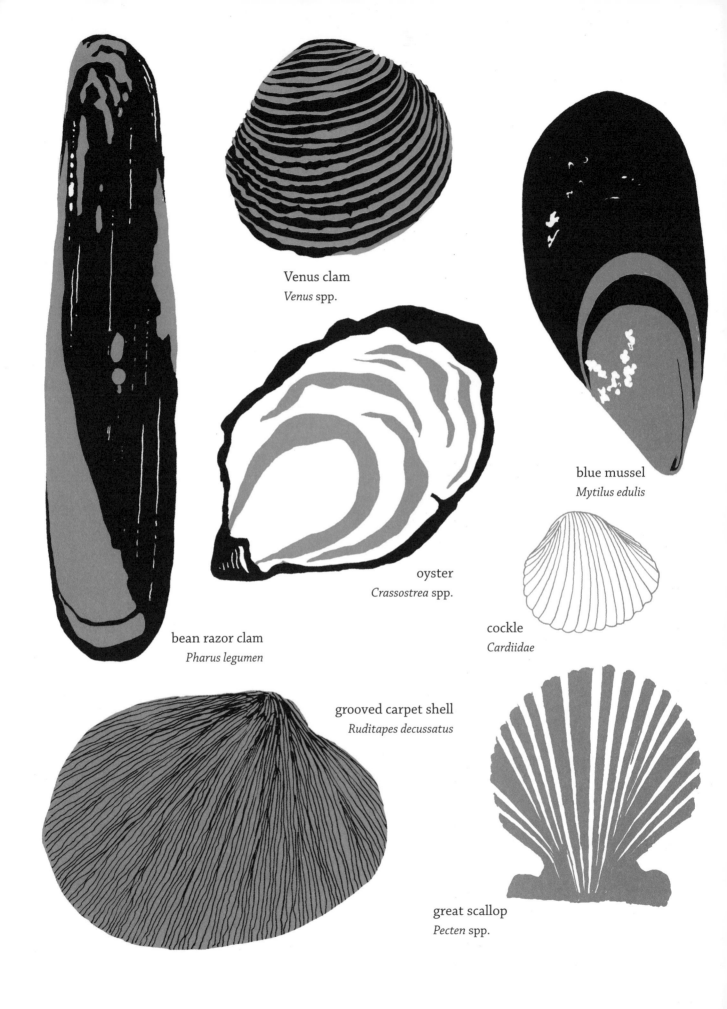

Venus clam
Venus spp.

blue mussel
Mytilus edulis

oyster
Crassostrea spp.

cockle
Cardiidae

bean razor clam
Pharus legumen

grooved carpet shell
Ruditapes decussatus

great scallop
Pecten spp.

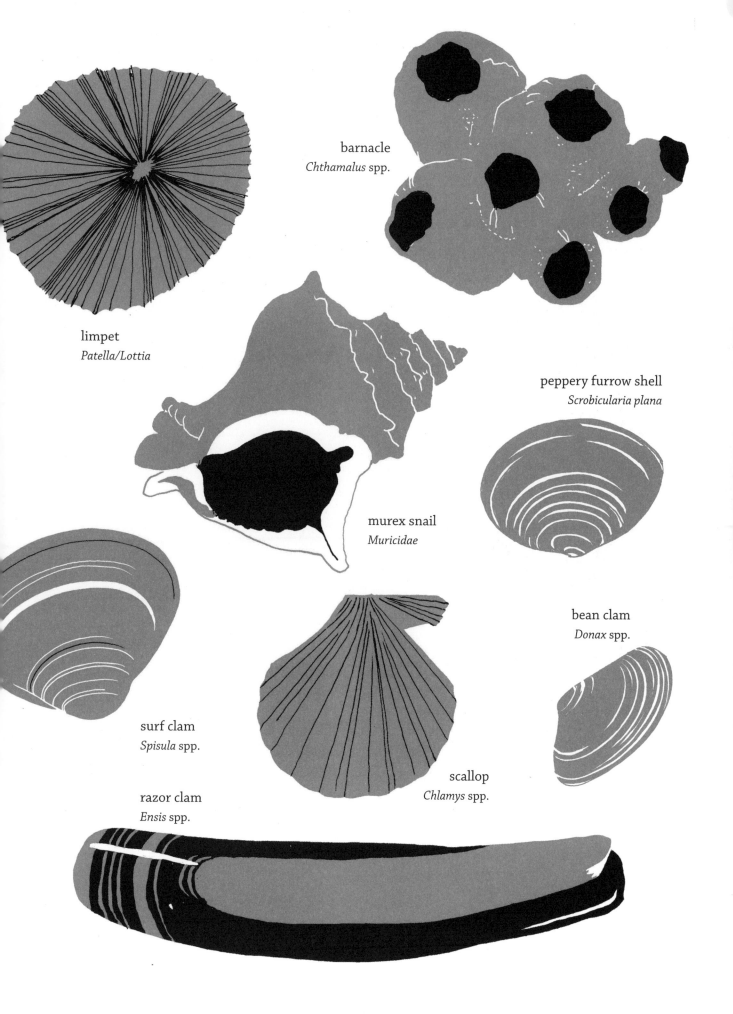

barnacle
Chthamalus spp.

limpet
Patella/Lottia

peppery furrow shell
Scrobicularia plana

murex snail
Muricidae

bean clam
Donax spp.

surf clam
Spisula spp.

scallop
Chlamys spp.

razor clam
Ensis spp.

Do the animals in tide pools eat one another?

Like in any ecosystem, there are predators and prey in a tide pool. But even the hungriest predator doesn't eat everything in front of it. (When you're hungry, you don't eat everything in the fridge all at once!) And don't forget that tide pools are temporary—when the tide comes back in, the animals that were trapped there can finally get out and move somewhere else. What you find in a tide pool can differ a lot from day to day.

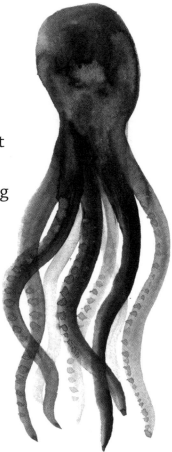

There are real stars in tide pools!

Starfish are the real stars of tide pools. They're pretty, colorful, and—strange as this might seem—they're predators, which means that they hunt other small animals, such as mussels. Plus, they have a peculiar characteristic: when they lose one of their arms, a new one grows back in the same place. But don't pull them off! Their arms take a long time (months, or even years) to grow, and a starfish is more vulnerable to diseases when it loses one.

Another of the "stars" of a tide pool is the octopus. With its eight arms, it can get to all corners of the tide pool, looking for food or escaping from whoever wants to snack on it. Octopuses are very intelligent animals, and they squirt ink to confuse animals that threaten them.

✳

Shall we go tide-pooling?

- -

When biologists make a record of the animals they find in tide pools, it's called a field survey. Even if you're not going to do a scientific study, when you look into each tide pool, you can always learn a lot!

Important tips:

- The seaweed that covers rocks can be slippery. You should also be careful not to cut your feet on shells, so don't go barefoot: it's best to wear an old pair of sneakers (that you don't mind getting wet with seawater).

- Take a net with you to help catch animals and put them in a bucket of seawater for a few minutes. This will make it easier to identify the animals you see, using the pictures in this chapter.

- If you catch an octopus, be careful with the ink! And if you catch a starfish, be careful not to pull off any of its arms.

To "fish" for crabs:

- Some animals in tide pools, like crabs, are able to stay out of the water for a long time. You can try to "fish" them to observe them. To do this, use a net, a bucket, and bait (for example, a piece of mackerel or sardine).

- Go "fishing" at low tide. Look for crabs in the darkest parts of tide pools, underneath laminaria (reddish-brown seaweed) and underneath stones.

- Put bait inside your net. Move the bait slowly and pull gently when the crab bites, but, don't forget, your net should already be in the water to avoid sudden movements!

Warning: It's really important that when you're done, you release the animals back into the tide pool they came from.

Have fun tide-pooling!

What's out there beyond the horizon?

When we're at the beach and look out over the ocean, the ocean seems endless. But it does have an end—and this end is another continent. That continent is a very long way away, however, beyond the "curve" of the earth, and that's why you can't see it, even with most powerful binoculars.

Let's go and visit an island

Islands are very special places for biologists because they're sometimes home to species that don't exist anywhere else, and also because lots of marine animals—like seals and seabirds—choose them as a place to breed. Visiting an island with colonies of seabirds or seals is not always easy, but it's not impossible. And it's an unforgettable journey, since it almost always involves a boat ride, during which you can see lots of animals, such as sea turtles, dolphins, or, if you're lucky, a whale.

There are lots of islands that can be easily visited, and the best time to do this is in summer. Depending on the island you visit, you'll be able to find different species.

Gulls are the most common inhabitants, but there can also be terns, petrels and shearwaters. Petrels are rarer and harder to spot—many of them only visit the island during the night (especially on the darkest, moonless nights), to avoid being seen by predators.

If you stay overnight there you might be lucky enough to hear a petrel—some species make an unmistakable sound, and you'll certainly notice if one flies by!

What animals live in the ocean where I swim?

Fortunately, in most places, we don't have to share the ocean with any dangerous animals when we go swimming. But you could stand on a weever or be stung by a jellyfish. But these things don't happen too often, and when we go for a dip, most of the animals around us are harmless. And there are lots of them! Garfish, white seabream, mackerel, and sand smelts, to give just a few examples.

✳ Tips for a different kind of dip

- -

Equipment: A mask, a snorkel, and flippers.

Have you ever tried to open your eyes underneath the water?
If you have, you found out that it's not always easy to see much, and sooner or later, your eyes start to burn because of the salt.

Here are some tips to help you make the most of your dip:
- Get a diving mask so you can see a new underwater world!
- Even better, if you have a snorkel to help you breathe, you can explore without having to come to the surface all the time.
- With flippers, you can swim faster. You'll be able to swim for longer and see more fish, seaweed, anemones, octopuses, and much more.

Warning: Never swim alone! You should always be accompanied by an adult, and never lose sight of them when you're underneath the water. Don't try to catch the animals you find. Some can cause allergic reactions or even bite, so the golden rule is look at everything, but touch nothing!

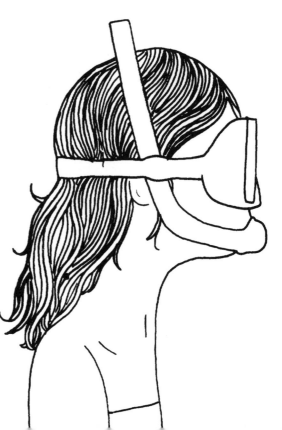

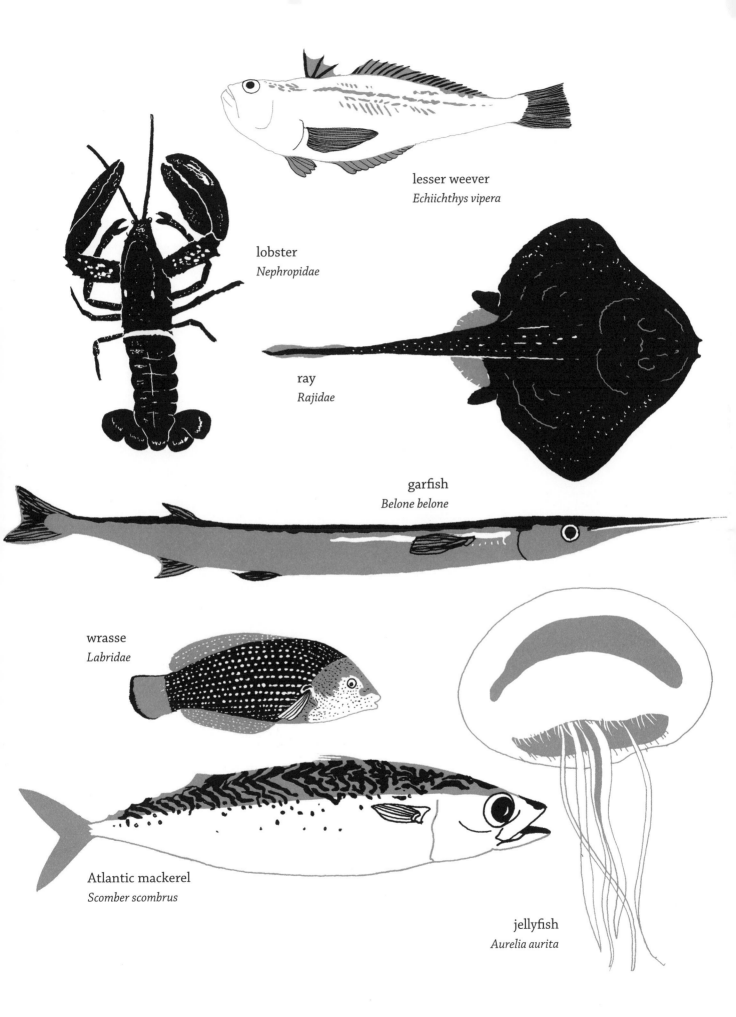

lesser weever
Echiichthys vipera

lobster
Nephropidae

ray
Rajidae

garfish
Belone belone

wrasse
Labridae

Atlantic mackerel
Scomber scombrus

jellyfish
Aurelia aurita

Why don't animals in the ocean drown?

Unlike mammals, which breathe through their lungs, most marine animals breathe through gills (or branchiae), which allow them to breathe the oxygen that is dissolved in water. When the animals are out of the water, they're unable to breathe, because they can't get the oxygen they need to live from the air.

Birds go to the beach, too

Birds also like the beach. They don't go there to sunbathe or swim in the ocean—they go to eat. Buried in the damp sand of low tide or hidden in small tide pools are hundreds of small clams, worms, shrimps, and crabs that serve as food for many species. The birds that often show up for the feast are sanderlings and ruddy turnstones, but you might also see gray plovers, whimbrels, and even purple sandpipers. And, of course, gulls!

And where are all those birds when we don't see them in the summer?

Most of them only like to go to the beach in winter. When spring comes, almost all of them travel to latitudes farther north (we say they migrate—look again at the chapter on birds), and they only come back the following autumn.

Coastal birds

There are lots of species of birds that like eating on the mudbanks that are exposed at low tide. When the tide starts to come in they fly away to sheltered areas, where they're protected from the cold, wind, and predators, until the tide goes out again.

Some of these species are well-known to all of us, such as gulls, terns, and sandpipers. Others are less well-known, but that doesn't make them any less beautiful. Estuaries and deltas are excellent places to see them. Find out which is closest to your house and plan a visit. The best times of year are the months of September and May.

ruddy turnstone

herring gull
Larus argentatus

Kentish/snowy plover
Charadrius alexandrinus/nivosus

heron
Ardea spp.

mallard
Anas platyrhynchos

great white egret
Ardea alba

avocet
Recurvirostra avosetta

great cormorant
Phalacrocorax carbo

whimbrel
Numenius phaeopus

sanderling
Calidris alba

spoonbill
Platalea leucorodia

gray plover
Pluvialis squatarola

black-headed gull
Larus ridibundus

UP IN SPACE!

THE STARS, THE MOON, AND THE SUN

The questions we can ask about the moon and the stars are as infinite as the sky itself. Scientists have managed to find answers for some questions; for others, however, there are only possibilities.

When the sun sets and the temperature drops, there's still a lot waiting for us outside . . .

So put on a jacket, listen to the sounds of the night, and watch the sky.

Let's begin our journey . . .

"Celestial bodies" are everything that exists in space—the moon, the sun, other stars, planets, asteroids, etc.

Because they're closer, the celestial bodies we know best are those in our own solar system. This is where Earth is, spinning around the sun, along with seven other planets.

(1) Mercury **(2)** Venus **(3)** Earth **(4)** Mars **(5)** Jupiter **(6)** Saturn **(7)** Uranus **(8)** Neptune **(9)** The Sun

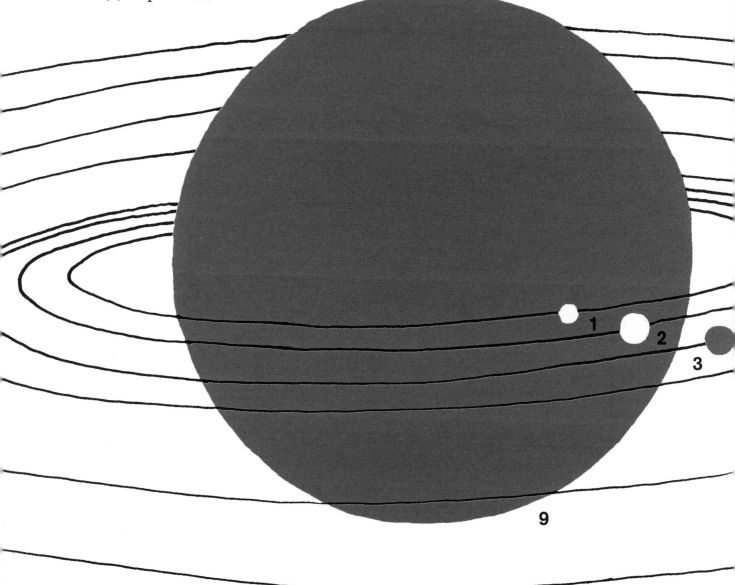

What planets can we see from Earth?

Some planets in the solar system are only observable with the help of a telescope. But others, especially the ones that are closest or biggest, can be seen with the naked eye (i.e., without the help of a telescope), as is the case with Mercury, Venus, Mars, Jupiter, and Saturn.

Because they're between us and the sun, Mercury and Venus can be seen at nightfall and the beginning of the night as well as at the end of the night and daybreak. Venus is the star that is most clearly visible at dusk or dawn—hence, its nicknames the Morning Star and the Evening Star.

To learn to tell a star from a planet, read "Lie in the dark . . . and look at the sky!" later in this chapter.

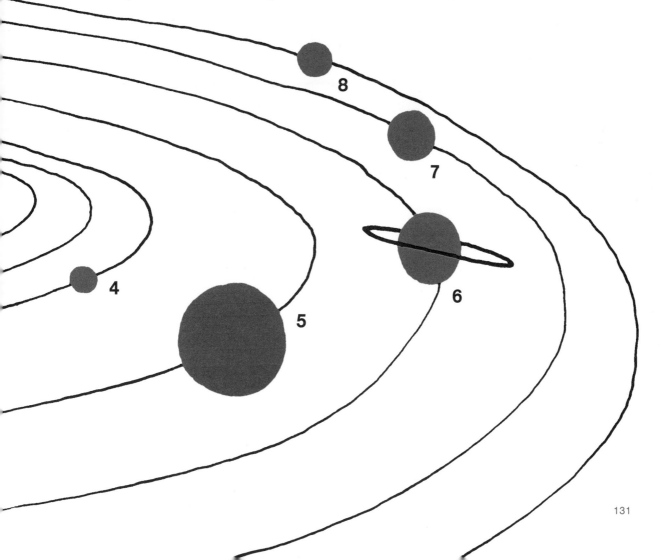

What are stars made of?

Stars are made of the lightest substance in existence: hydrogen.

In the center of a star is a kind of giant cauldron where hydrogen burns throughout the star's life. (Yes, stars are born, and they die, too . . .) The hydrogen turns into another substance called helium, which is a little bit heavier but still very light. (Yes, helium—the same stuff that's used to fill balloons.) Most of the light we receive from stars is produced in these "cauldrons"!

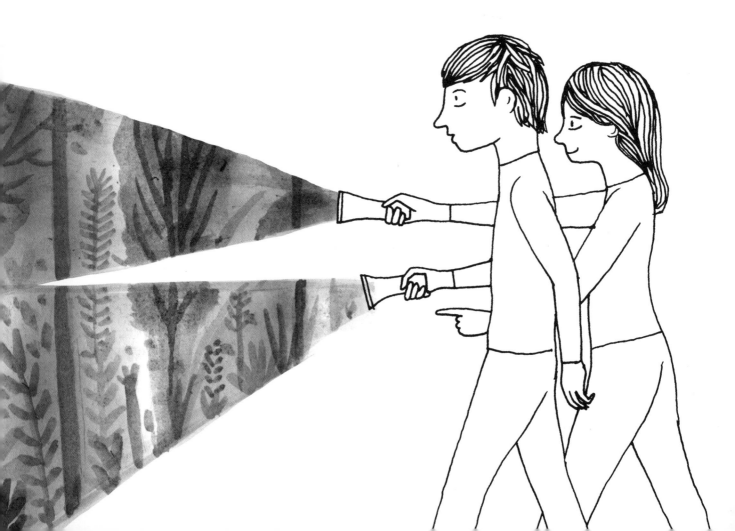

How many stars are there in the sky?

There are small stars, medium stars (like the sun), and giant stars. There are also different colored stars: red ones (which are the coldest), white ones, blue ones (which are the hottest) . . . Scientists don't know the exact number of stars out there, but they do know that there are lots and lots—many more than the grains of sand that exist on all the beaches on our planet.

Why does it look like there aren't any stars during the day?

That's because the light that reaches us from stars is so pale that as soon as the sun appears on the horizon, it blots out all the other stars and makes it look like there's no starry sky during the daytime! But the stars are indeed still there . . .

● ●
Go out for a flashlight walk

- - - - - - - - - - - -

A flashlight or head-lamp is enough to light your way during a nighttime walk.

If you go with younger brothers and sisters or younger friends, you might want to hold their hands . . . For little kids, the dark can be scary—but also exciting!

Listen to all the nighttime noises. (If you get scared, sing or whistle to yourself.)

Imitate an owl

- - - - - - - - - - - -

You can try to get a recording of owls and play it when you're in the countryside. You'll see that other birds will reply to you!

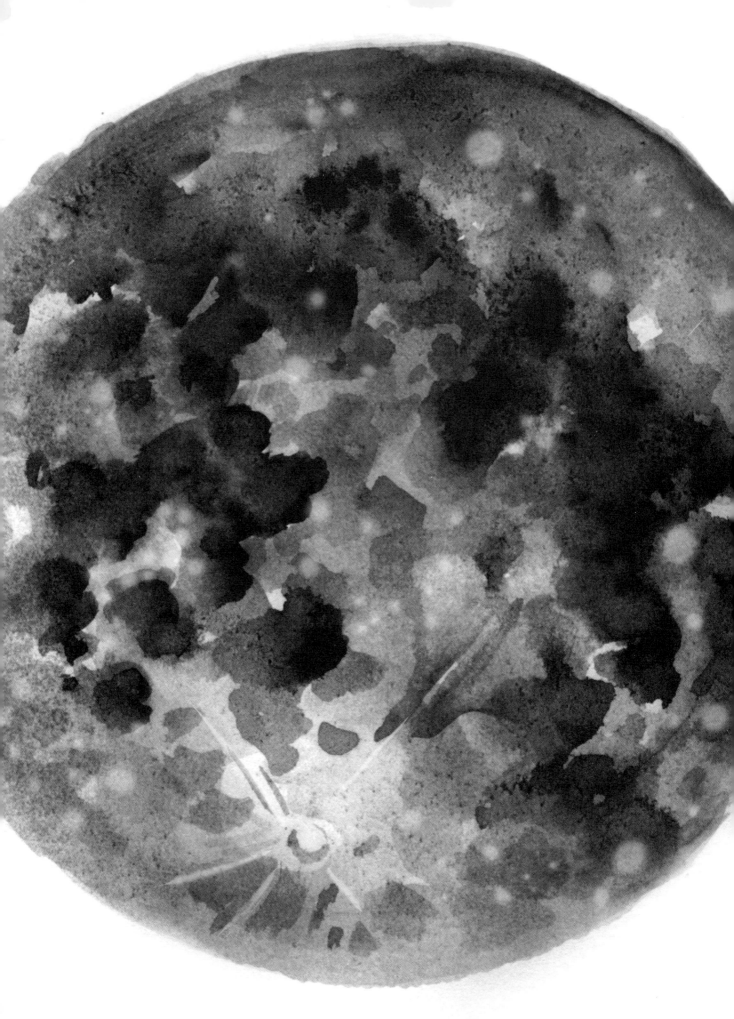

Next stop: the moon

The moon is a sphere almost 2,200 mi (3,500 km) in diameter, and it's Earth's natural satellite, which means it goes around our planet.

What is the moon made of?

The moon formed millions and millions of years ago. It's made of rock, just like Earth, and it might even be Earth's "child"—it could be a chunk of our planet!

This model of the moon's formation proposes that millions and millions of years ago, a very large object hit the Earth, and the impact made bits of our planet fly off. Later, these chunks stuck to the object that hit Earth, and this was the beginning of the new celestial body that began to gravitate around us.

Does the moon have its own light?

The moon isn't a star, and thus, it doesn't emit light. The light we see coming from the moon is called moonlight, and it's actually the light of the sun reflected off the moon's surface.

If you look carefully when the moon isn't full (try using binoculars to do this), you can see the part that isn't lit up by the sun.

Make an animation of the moon!

- - - - - - - - - - - - - - -

Using a pad of paper, try to make an animation showing how the moon moves. To achieve this effect (just like in an old-fashioned animation), you have to draw its movement, stage by stage, with each stage on a different page in the pad of paper. When you've finished, flick the pages quickly and watch the moon move: the moon revolving around Earth, Earth spinning, etc.

Note: To help you, look for images on the Internet that show the various stages of the moon.

- - - - - - - - - - - - - - -

Why don't we always see the moon?

The moon isn't always visible because it never stays still—it constantly revolves around Earth, taking 27 days and 7 hours to complete a circuit of our planet. While the moon spins around us, we see different areas illuminated by the sun, and there's a period when we can't see the illuminated part because its back is facing us.

An interesting fact: The moon always shows the same side! This happens because its rotation is synchronized—the time it takes to rotate is the same as the time it takes to complete an orbit of Earth.

How fast does the moon move?

The moon moves very fast! The moon orbits Earth at a speed of 2,287 mph (3,683 kph).

Is there life on the moon?

Nope. There are no animals, no plants, and no other kind of living things. As a matter of fact, no form of life has been discovered outside our planet. (Scientists have never found any aliens!)

Even though there's no life there, the moon is very important for the living things on our planet: some animals are more active on nights when the moon is full because they use moonlight to hunt; others only dare to leave their burrows at new moon, in the darkness, so they won't be hunted. Small sea turtles born on the beach use moonlight to find their way back to the ocean. It's also thanks to the moon that there are tides. (Learn why in the "Oceans, Beaches, and Tide Pools" chapter.) And there are lots of animals and plants that need the tides to live.

What kind of moon is there tonight?

On a cloudless night, you can look for the moon in the sky and try to see which phase it's in. Finding the moon might not be easy—if you live in a city, it'd be best to go to an area where you can see a good portion of the sky (in case the moon is hiding behind a building, etc.). If the sky is very cloudy, you can try another day: the moon is much easier to find when there are no clouds.

To identify the phase of the moon, compare it with these images:

New moon
When the moon is between Earth and the sun, the sun only illuminates the side of the moon that "has its back to us." In other words, this is the phase in which it's most difficult to see.

Waxing moon
This is the phase in which the moon is midway between new moon and full moon and is a D shape.

Full moon
When the moon is on the opposite side of Earth from the sun, we see the whole moon illuminated by the sun.

Waning moon
In this phase, the moon is midway between full moon and new moon and is a C shape.

If you can't find a moon at all . . . does that mean it's new moon?

Not always. It might just mean that the moon has already set—there's a time when the moon rises and another when it sets (just like the sun). This time changes according to the phase:

○ The **full moon** rises at the end of the afternoon and sets in the early morning: you can find it all night.

○ The **new moon** rises at dawn and sets at dusk: you can see it, very faintly, during the day.

○ The **waning moon** rises at

137

Lie in the dark . . . and look at the sky!

On a night when there's a new moon, lie on the ground and observe the sky.

As soon as you've gotten used to the darkness, you'll start to see thousands of stars and the odd planet.

Stars twinkle, their light appearing to flicker instead of being constant; planets, on the other hand, don't seem to twinkle and are more "fixed." If you look carefully, it won't take long for you to see some lights slowly crossing the sky, too. These are artificial satellites—devices that orbit Earth and are used for telecommunications, for example. Don't confuse them with "shooting stars," which aren't real stars—they're meteorites. If you're lucky enough to see one of those, don't forget to make a wish!

If you want to know more, take a pocket star guide with you.

Has anyone ever been to the sun?

Nope! They'd be burned to death immediately—the temperature on the surface of the sun is almost 10,000 degrees Fahrenheit (6,000 degrees Celsius). The sun emits light constantly, and this light takes eight minutes to reach Earth. So when we look at the sun, we see it as it was eight minutes ago! This light is the source of energy for all plants and animals on our planet.

Why does the sun rise and set every day?

The sun looks as if it moves in the sky: it rises in the east and sets in the west. But in fact, it's not the sun that moves—it's our planet that moves!

Earth revolves around the sun, but it also spins on its own axis (twirling like a top). Earth takes 24 hours (a whole day) to complete a spin. This movement is called rotation, and the rotation means that the sun illuminates different parts of our planet throughout the day. Earth takes about 365 days to complete an orbit around the sun.

Is sunlight really yellow?

Nope! The sun's light is white because it is made of all the colors of the rainbow. (Did you know that white light is a combination of all colors?) The sun looks yellow to us because the different colors of light don't reach us in the same way—blue and violet stop on the way and "spread out" through Earth's atmosphere—this is why the sky looks blue! The sunlight that reaches us has all the colors mixed together, except the bluish ones, which makes the yellow color that we see.

Why does the sun look much bigger than other stars?

The sun isn't really bigger than all the other stars out there. It's actually medium-sized—there are some stars that are much bigger and others that are much smaller . . . The sun looks bigger than other stars we see at night because it's much closer to us: it's about 90 million miles (150 million kilometers) away. This may seem really far, but the second-closest star to us (Proxima Centauri) is much, much farther away—25 trillion miles (40 trillion kilometers)!

● ● ● ● ● ●

Use the light of the sun (and the shadows it creates)

Let's finish up with some activities that will let you feel the power of the sun and the beauty of shadows . . .

Don't miss sunrise or sunset!
Sunrise and sunset are two of the most magical moments in nature. To see the dawn (sunrise), find a high place, with good visibility and look toward the horizon in the east (the direction in which the sun rises).

To see the dusk (sunset), you'll have to know which way west is.

Look on the Internet to find the exact time of sunrise and sunset in your city.

- -

Paint the sky at sunset
Choose a day when there aren't many clouds. Get everything ready: paints, paintbrushes, paper (or a canvas). As soon as the sun begins to set, start working! Take inspiration from the colors you see.

- -

Check out your shadow
Stretch out a sheet or a piece of paper and stick it on a wall facing the sun. Now step between the sun and the white surface to see your shadow. Get a friend to draw your shadow, and then you can draw your friend's. Don't just stand there—try out funny positions!

Colorful shadows
Use sheets of colored acetate or transparent colored paper to see colorful projections! Just hold up the sheet and see what happens when the sun shines through it and projects a shadow on the ground. You could cut out different shapes of the acetate or paper (for instance, an umbrella or a watering can).

- -

Observe the power of the sun
Sunlight is powerful. Put various materials on a tray (or objects made from different materials). Try a piece of wood, cloth, plastic, rubber, etc. Put the tray in the sun and observe what happens after 1 day, after 5 days, after 10 days, after a month . . .

- -

Draw light and shadow
Look for an area under a tree with light and shade. Move a sheet of paper along the ground to find pretty shapes. When you find some, draw the outlines on the paper.

Note: Never look directly at the sun—it's very dangerous for your eyes.
And don't forget to wear a hat and use sunscreen if you're in the sun for a long time.

The sky offers us unforgettable sights every day: clouds travel across it, rain falls from it, the wind blows in it, and small and large storms form in it . . .

Let's take a good look at it!

What is the sky made of?

The sky is the part of the atmosphere or of space that can be seen from Earth. We say that both clouds and stars are in the sky . . .

What is the atmosphere?
The atmosphere is what we call air.

It's made up of gases, mainly nitrogen (around 78 percent) and oxygen (around 21 percent). There are also smaller quantities of water, dust, pollen . . .

Why doesn't the atmosphere disappear into space?
The atmosphere has a low density and could go on rising constantly until it's lost in the universe. This doesn't happen because the force of gravity keeps it in place, in the same way that it keeps us on the ground.

What's Earth's atmosphere for?
Earth's atmosphere protects living things from the sun's radiation, helps to keep Earth's temperature mild, transports water from one region to another, and contains gases (such as oxygen) that are essential to life.

✳

Try to see the air!

- - - - - - - - - - - - - - - -

On a sunny afternoon, find a window where sunlight enters directly. Lie on the floor underneath the window and quietly observe the rays as they enter. Once your eyes get used to it, you'll see that light is reflected off small particles of dust in the air. Sunlight makes these particles visible. Many other particles—which are even smaller—are there as well.

What you've got there is a bit of air, visible air.

- - - - - - - - - - - - - - - -

Is there as much air down here as there is up there?

Closer to the surface of Earth, the air is more dense; the farther you get from Earth, the less dense the air is. This means that as we move away from the surface, there is less air. This is why it's harder for us to breathe at the summit of very high mountains!

Does the moon have an atmosphere?

The moon we see from Earth doesn't have an atmosphere because it has very little gravity, but many of the other planets in the solar system and their respective moons do have atmospheres. Even so, none compares to ours!

Why is the sky blue during the day?

The sun emits light of all colors. The mixture of all these colors makes the color white. (This is why we say that sunlight is white.)

During the day, tiny particles in the atmosphere spread out the part of the light that corresponds to the color blue more than others. This is the color that reaches our eyes, which is why the sky looks blue to us.

Rainbows are amazing!

You can see a rainbow when the sun's rays pass through drops of water and are refracted and reflected—the water droplets change the direction of rays of light.

But why do we see rainbows as colors?
Sunlight is made up of all the colors . . . all the colors of the rainbow! But because we normally see all these colors together, we see sunlight as white.

However, when sunlight passes through a drop of water, it's as if the drop is a machine able to separate light into its colors: at that moment, the solar spectrum divides, and all the colors that were previously mixed are visible.

Is it possible to see two rainbows at the same time?
Yes, this does sometimes happen. In these cases, above the main rainbow we see a slightly larger and less bright rainbow. This happens when drops of water reflect the sun's rays doubly.

If you look carefully, you'll notice that the second rainbow has its colors in the opposite order than the first one.

Where should you stand?
To be able to see a rainbow, the sun has to be behind you and there have to be raindrops in the direction you're looking.

✻ Learn the colors of the rainbow

Isaac Newton was the first scientist to manage to separate the colors of sunlight, and back then, he saw only five colors . . . There were other people who saw only six colors . . . Today, though, almost everyone accepts that the rainbow contains seven colors, always in this order: red (on the outside of the rainbow), orange, yellow, green, blue, indigo, and violet (on the inside of the rainbow).

A tip: To learn the sequence of the colors by heart, you can use the acronym Roy G. Biv: imagine a character with that name! The letters also stand for the colors of the rainbow: Red, Orange, Yellow, Green, Blue, Indigo, Violet.

What a lovely nimbostratus . . .

What are clouds?

Clouds are formed by a collection of tiny drops of water or ice crystals. These drops are so small and so light that they float in the air without falling. Clouds become visible in the sky when billions of drops of water group together.

The scientists' code

The system that scientists use to classify clouds was first developed by an English amateur meteorologist, a pharmacist named Luke Howard, in 1803.

In 1887, Ralph Abercrombie and Hugo Hildebrandsson generalized Howard's system, and the system today divides clouds into the following levels of altitude:

High-level clouds

These are the highest clouds, found at altitudes above 4 mi (7 km). Formed of ice crystals, they are fine, white, and shiny, and indicate good weather.

Mid-level clouds

Found at mid-level altitudes, between 1 and 4 mi (2 and 7 km). They're normally in layers, and bluish or grayish in color. They give rise to rain.

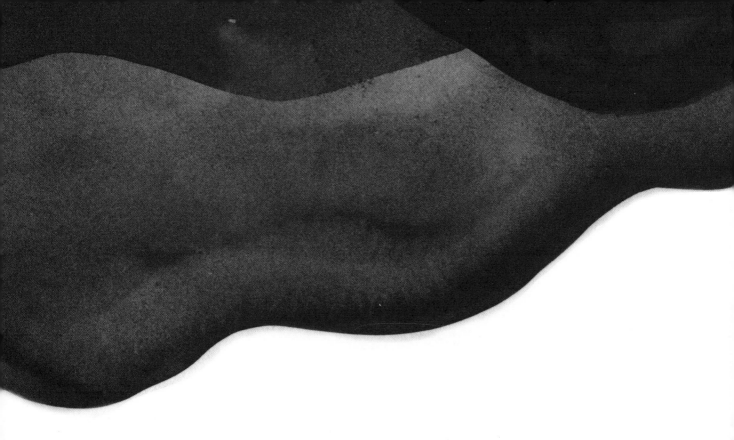

Low-level clouds
These are the lowest clouds, found at altitudes of less than 1 mi (2 km).

Vertically developed clouds
The base can be between altitudes of 650 ft and 2 mi (200 m and 3 km).
These clouds can extend upward for up to 6 mi (9 km)!
They give rise to heavy rainstorms.

The 10 types of cloud that exist are grouped into these categories (see the following pages).

Where do the names of clouds come from?
Scientists name clouds using combinations of words that come from Latin:

- Stratus/Strato—flat, crushed, in layers
- Cumulus/Cumulo—bulky, like a cauliflower
- Cirrus/Cirro—fine, curl of hair
- Alto—mid-level
- Nimbus/Nimbo—cloud that brings rain

High-level

(1) <u>Cirrus</u> are the most common high clouds.

(2) <u>Cirrostratus</u> are so fine that they let sun and moonlight pass through.

(3) <u>Cirrocumulus</u> are small, round clouds that look like a thick rope. They appear more in winter and indicate good but cold weather.

Mid-level

(4) <u>Altostratus</u> cover almost the whole sky, and where they are least dense, they let us see the sun like a white disc.

(5) <u>Altocumulus</u> look like little sheep in the sky. If you see them on a warm, humid morning, get ready for a thunderstorm in the afternoon!

Low-level

(6) <u>Nimbostratus</u> have a thick, dark base. When we see them, we might say, "It smells like rain."

(7) <u>Stratus</u> look like mist, but higher. They sometimes give rise to rain showers.

(8) <u>Stratocumulus</u> are gray and fluffy. They rarely give rise to rain.

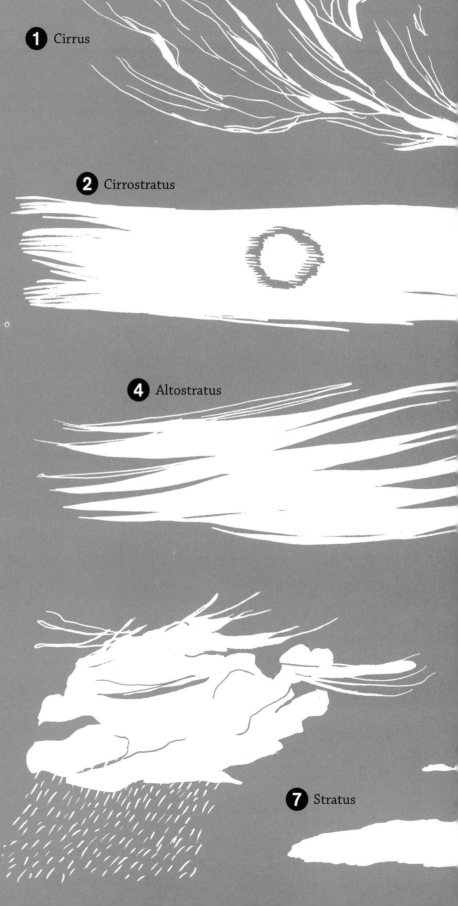

1 Cirrus

2 Cirrostratus

4 Altostratus

7 Stratus

6 Nimbostratus

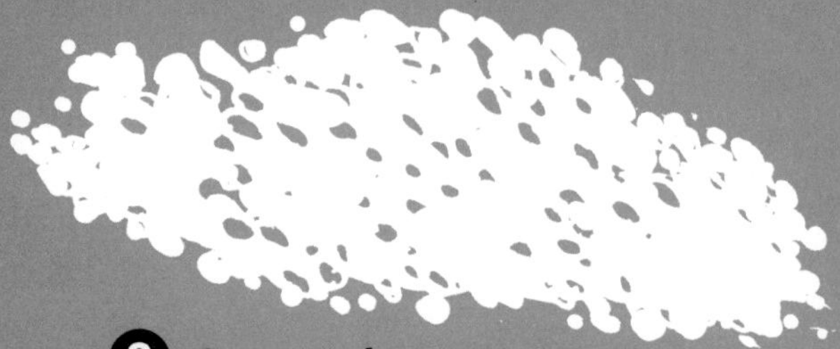

3 Cirrocumulus

Vertically developed

(9) <u>Cumulus</u> are clouds with a specific shape: the base is flat and the tops are rounded. They're "good weather" clouds, but can easily change . . .

(10) <u>Cumulonimbus</u> are huge clouds that can look like mushrooms. They're known as storm clouds.

Altocumulus

9 Cumulus

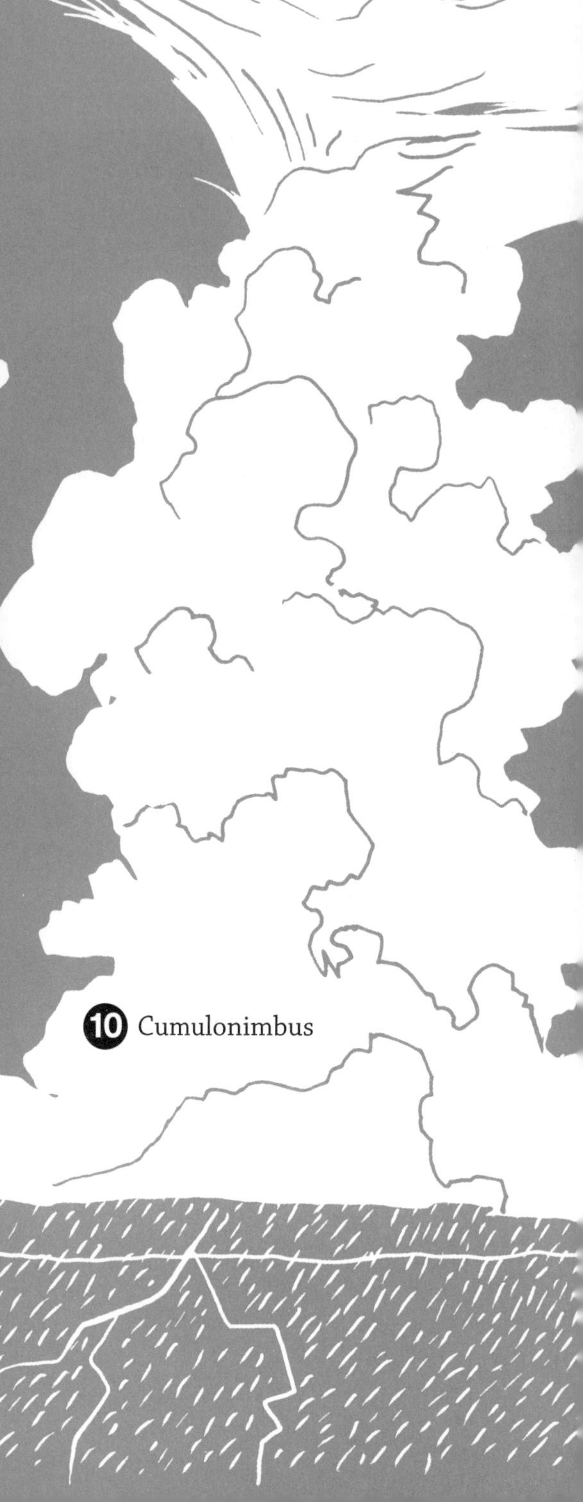

10 Cumulonimbus

8 Stratocumulus

Here comes the rain!

How do clouds form?

Everyone knows there's water in the air. But water in the air (which you can't see) isn't liquid water—it's water in gas form, or water vapor.

When the air, loaded with water vapor, rises in the atmosphere and meets cold air, the water suspended in it condenses into millions of droplets and forms clouds. These droplets join others, growing bigger and "heavier." And then, ping! It starts raining.

What makes the clouds move?

Clouds are pushed by the wind, of course! The highest clouds are pushed by giant currents of air and can move at over 100 mph (160 kph).

What is wind?

Wind is air that's moving.

And wind is due mainly to the sun's energy. Do you know why?

The sun heats the atmosphere differently in different regions of the planet. These differences in temperature and pressure form wind, with air moving from areas where the pressure is higher to areas where the pressure is lower.

✳ What to do on a rainy day?

- -

Rainy days don't have to be boring!

Here's a list of fun things you can do with a raincoat and pair of rain boots.

Draw the wind
Is the wind visible? Sometimes it is; sometimes it isn't. Can you pin it down on paper using pens or pencils? Try representing it in various ways. Let yourself get carried away by the storm!

Draw animals that fly
There are lots of them: butterflies, mosquitoes, bees, birds (and even fish!).

If you like, you can draw yourself flying among them.

Have a cloud race
Choose a cloud in the sky. Tell your friends to do the same with other clouds. Now watch the wind push your clouds, and see which wins the race!

Jump in a rain puddle!
Only if the puddle isn't very deep, of course—and if you're wearing the right shoes.

Go *splish, splash, splosh* until a grown-up comes along and says: "That's enough!"

You can also try throwing small stones into puddles . . . (No big rocks, though, okay?)

Organize a paper boat regatta
If there's a lot of water running down the street, use one of the streams to organize a race with paper boats. Use pages from magazines: the thicker and shinier the better. Be sure to clean up what's left at the end.

Make rain soup
Put a bucket in the rain until it's full. Then add leaves, stones, flowers, seeds, whatever you find . . . Mix everything with a long stick. What does it smell like?

What does rain do to colors?
Color in several sheets of paper. (You can use pens, colored pencils, or watercolors.) Put the sheets of paper in the rain (on the clothesline, on the porch, in the yard). Look at what happens. You can also get it to rain on a drawing you've already done.

159

✳

**Go out into the street
on a really windy day**

– – – – – – – – – – – – – – –

Pick a windy day. Watch how
everything moves: the trees,
the grass, the clothes and
sheets on the clothesline,
people's hair. Close your
eyes and feel the wind
blowing on you.

(If it's cold, make sure to cover
up your head and ears.)

GLOSSARY

A

Adaptation
The way an organism becomes more suited to its environment.

Androecium
The male part of a flower. It is formed by the stamens, which produce the pollen.

Aquifer
Sources of underground water.

Atmosphere
The layer of gases that surrounds a planet. The most abundant gases in Earth's atmosphere are nitrogen and oxygen.

B

Biodiversity
The variety and abundance of living organisms that exist in a region.

Botany
The branch of biology that studies plants.

Branchiae
The organs that some animals, such as fish, use to breathe. In fish, these can also be called gills. The larvae of amphibians have branchiae, which they lose when they become adults and develop lungs.

C

Calyx
The sepals of a flower, which protect the petals and reproductive organs.

Cambium
The layer of tissue that builds xylem and phloem.

Celestial body
Everything that exists in space—the moon, the sun, other stars, planets, asteroids, etc.

Cell
The basic structure of living organisms. Animals and plants, for example, are made up of many millions of cells. Cells are so small that they can only be seen with the help of a microscope.

Classification
The arrangement of animals into groups according to their similarities and relationships with one aother.

Colony (breeding)

A concentration of animals (birds, for example) that make their nests near one another.

Commercial

Something which is aimed at making a profit.

Condensation

Passage from a gaseous to a liquid state.

Continental drift

The name for the movement of the large plates of rock that form Earth's crust.

Corolla

A flower's petals, which normally have the function of attracting pollinators.

Colony

A concentration of animals (birds, for example) that make their nests near one another.

Crown (of a tree)

The top part of a tree, which is made up of branches and is where the leaves, flowers, and fruit are found.

Cultivation

The act of using land to grow and care for plants, such as when farmers prepare land to grow crops.

D

Deciduous

Used to describe the leaves of plants that fall at a given time of year.

Density

A measurement of the mass of a substance per unit of volume. If something is less dense than a liquid it is sitting on, then it will float. If something is more dense than a liquid it is sitting on, it will sink. This word can also describe how compact or concentrated something is.

Diameter

The length of a straight line through the center of a circular object or sphere.

Dioecious

Used to describe a plant that has male and female flowers.

E

Ecology

The branch of biology that studies the relationships between organisms and the environment that surrounds them.

Ecosystem

The sum of all the organisms that live in a region, the environment that surrounds them, and all their relationships.

Endemic species

A species that only exists in a given region and does not spontaneously occur anywhere else.

Evaporation

The way in which water changes from a liquid state to a gas or vapor.

Evergreen

A plant that holds onto its green leaves throughout the year.

Evolution

Changes in the hereditary characteristics of a species that can occur from one generation to another. This process means that species change and diversify over time, adapting to the changing environment and giving rise to others.

Extinction

The disappearance of a species. We say that a species is extinct when all the organisms in that species have died.

F

Fauna

The animals of a particular region or time period.

Fertilization

The union of male and female reproductive cells, giving rise to an ovum, the beginning of a new living being.

Flora

The plants of a particular region or time period.

Fossil

The name given to the remains of plants or animals that are found in layers of the Earth from thousands or millions of years ago.

Fungi

A group of simple organisms which eat decaying material or other living things.

G

Geology

The science that studies the Earth (the composition of rocks, the evolution of our planet, earthquakes, etc.).

Global warming

The gradual increase in a planet's temperature due to the trapping of the sun's heat in its atmosphere.

GPS

An abbreviation of *global positioning system*. This is a system that allows us to find our exact location using information sent to artificial satellites orbiting the Earth.

Gravitate

To be attracted towards—or move towards—something.

Gravity

The name of a force which attracts a body towards the center of another body, such as the Earth.

Greenhouse gas

Gases which are responsible for global warming.

Gynoecium

A flower's carpels, its female reproductive organs. The carpels are formed of stigma, styles, and ovaries and can be free or joined together. The term *pistil* is commonly used to describe a free carpel or several carpels joined together. A flower can have one or many pistils.

H

Habitat
A location with the conditions necessary for the survival of a species.

Hardy
Being able to endure difficult conditions.

Hermaphrodite
An organism that has both male and female reproductive organs.

I

Igneous rock
A type of rock which forms when magma cools and solidifies.

Inflorescence
The form in which flowers group together on a plant. There are different kinds of inflorescence: raceme, capitulum, amentum, panicle, corymb, umbel, and spadix.

L

Larva
The state of some animals before they become adults. Larvae do not reproduce. They can look like adults (as is the case with cockroaches), or they can look very different (as is the case with butterflies).

Latitude
A distance north or south of the Earth's equator.

Lava
Hot, liquid rock which erupts from a volcano.

M

Magma
Hot, liquid rock below the Earth's surface.

Marcescent
Used to describe leaves that, even though they are dead, do not fall from the plant until new leaves begin to grow.

Metamorphic rock
Rock which has been transformed by heat or pressure.

Meteorology
The science that studies the phenomena that occur in the atmosphere, in particular those related to the weather. (Meteorologists are the people who are able to predict if it will be sunny or rainy tomorrow.)

Mohs scale
A measurement of how easily a mineral is scratched by another.

Mollusk

A member of a group of invertebrate animals which have soft bodies and are usually covered in a shell.

Monoecious

Used to describe a plant that has male and female flowers on the same plant. This is different than a hermaphroditic plant, the flowers of which have both sexes.

(N)

Native species

A species that exists in a region and was not taken there artificially (i.e., by humans).

Nectar

A sugary liquid produced by flowers that is used to attract pollinators.

(O)

Orbit

The path followed by an object around another, such as a planet orbiting the sun.

Ovule

A female reproductive cell.

(P)

Permeable

Allowing liquid or gas to pass through it. The opposite of permeable is impermeable.

Phloem sap

A liquid formed of sugars and other nutrients, almost always produced by the leaves of plants.

Photosynthesis

The process whereby plants transform carbon dioxide (from the air) and water (absorbed through their roots) into glucose, with the help of the sun. Glucose is the plant's source of energy.

Pollen

Minute grains produced by the male organs of flowers (stamen) that carry the male reproductive cells. When these cells join with female reproductive cells (ovules), they give rise to seeds.

Pollination

The sexual act of plants, or the passage of pollen from stamen to the gynoecium. When this happens within a flower or between two flowers on the same plant, it is called self-pollination; when it happens between flowers on different plants, it is called cross-pollination.

Pollinators

Elements that help plants carry out pollination. They may be various kinds of animals such as insects, birds, or mammals, or agents that are not living things, such as the wind (anemophily) or water (hydrophily), or humans (artificial).

Porous

Having small holes, allowing liquid or air to pass through.

Predator

An animal that kills another animal in order to eat it.

Prey

An animal killed by another organism for food.

R

Radiation (ultraviolet)

These are rays of light from the sun (or other stars), but they are different than those that form colors. We aren't able to see ultraviolet rays (unlike other animals such as insects), but their harmful effects are well known—they cause sunburn when we don't protect our skin enough.

Refraction

Reproduction

The way living things produce other living things, their descendants, which continue the species. Reproduction can be sexual, when sex cells from two living things (female and male) come together, or asexual, when a single living thing produces another one exactly like it (such as when plants grow roots that produce other plants).

Respiration

The act of breathing, or the way organisms produce energy by taking in oxygen and glucose and releasing waste products.

S

Scientific name

All species of living things have a scientific name. This is formed of two parts: the first is the genus and must be written with a capital letter; the second is called the species. Both should be written in italics.

Sedimentary rock

Rocks that form as a result of sediment building up and compacting together.

Seismograph

Machines used by scientists to detect movements in the ground.

Sepal

The small green parts that protect a flower when it is still a bud.

Species

A group of organisms that is able to reproduce together and have fertile offspring.

Stamen

The male reproductive organs of a flower where pollen is stored.

Suber

The name give in botany to the bark of woody plants. It's the tissue that protects the plant and makes it waterproof.

Subterranean

Something which exists or occurs underground.

T

Transpiration
The way water moves up through a plant from its roots to its leaves, where it evaporates as water vapor.

V

Vulnerable species
A species at risk of extinction. This is one of the eight categories of threat used to classify species. The others are: *Extinct, Extinct in the Wild, Critically Endangered, Endangered, Near Threatened, Least Concern.* This classification is used internationally and is represented in the IUCN (International Union for the Conservation of Nature) Red List.

W

Waterline
The line that separates the surface of water from the depths below.

Water vapor
Water that exists in the atmosphere in the form of gas, usually as a result of evaporation.

Wave trough
The lowest part of a wave, between two wave crests.

Wave crest
The highest part of a wave.

Wave height
The distance between a wave trough and wave crest.

Wavelength
The distance between two wave crests or two wave troughs.

X

Xylem
The tissue in vascular plants that transports xylem sap from the roots to the leaves.

Xylem Sap
A liquid made from water and mineral salts that, in vascular plants, is transported from the roots to other parts of the plant (generally the leaves) where it will be transformed into sugar.

TIMELINE
IMPORTANT DATES

350 BC (approx.)

The Greek philosopher Aristotle collects examples of fauna and flora to group them according to their characteristics. This is the first classification of living things that we know of.

1632

Birth of Benedict de Spinoza, the philosopher who understood nature as a continuation of God. For Spinoza, stones, animals, and plants all have a body and mind.

1735

The botanist Carl von Linné (known as Linnaeus) publishes the first edition of *Systema Naturae*—the system of classification used, even today, to classify living things according to what we call their scientific name.

1866

Ernst Haeckel first coins the term "ecology" to describe the study of the relationship between organisms and where they live. The word comes from the Greek "logos" (study) and "oikos" (home).

1872

In the United States, a bill is passed by Congress and signed into law by President Grant to create the world's first national park. Yellowstone National Park now comprises more than 2 million acres.

1895

The National Trust is founded in the UK to preserve outdoor spaces and prevent them from being built on. Today they are the UK's biggest land owner.

1915

In the UK, banker and expert naturalist Charles Rothschild holds a meeting to discuss his radical idea about saving places for nature. This meeting leads to the creation of the Society for the Promotion of Nature Reserves (SPNR) and signals the beginning of UK nature conservation.

1915

The Ecological Society of America, a nonprofit organization of scientists, is formed. Within two years, the ESA has 307 members.

1949

The book *A Sand County Almanac*, by Aldo Leopold, considered the father of wild ecology, is published. One of his most famous quotes is that we must learn to "think like a mountain."

1960

The British scientist James Lovelock proposes a theory known as the Gaia hypothesis, in which he presents the Earth as a unique living organism that is able to regulate itself in many ways.

1962

The biologist Rachel Carson publishes the book *Silent Spring*, in which she shows the risks of unregulated use of pesticides (DDT), especially to birds. This book led to a revolution in environmental laws.

1970

Earth Day is celebrated for the first time, on the April 22, in the United States.

1970

The European Council launches the European Year of Nature Conservation.

1971

Two of the world's most important environmental association are created: Friends of the Earth International and Greenpeace.

1973

Arne Naess introduces the concept of "deep ecology." For this Norwegian philosopher and mountaineer, nature is not just something to be manipulated for our benefit; it is a place for us to share, equally.

1973

The Convention on International Trade in Endangered Species of Wild Fauna and Flora (CITES) is approved, prohibiting the sale and purchase of thousands of endangered species.

1987

Introduction of the concept of "sustainable development," which demonstrates that the economy, people, and the environment must be linked, bearing the needs of future generations in mind.

1992

In Rio de Janeiro, world leaders meet to discuss the planet's environmental situation (at a conference known as ECO 92).

1997

Year of the Kyoto Protocol, which lays out goals for the reduction of global greenhouse gases, which are responsible for global warming.

2007/2009

The General Assembly of the United Nations dedicated the period between 2007 and 2009 for commemorations of International Year of Planet Earth.

2010

The United Nations declares 2010 International Year of Biodiversity.

If you want to know more . . .

Here are some organizations that work in the area of nature conservation or study. Check the websites to learn more about their activities:

Worldwide:

BGCI Botanic Gardens Conservation International
◉ www.bgci.org

BirdLife International
◉ www.birdlife.org

Conservation International
Environmental organisation
◉ www.conservation.org

Earth Island Institute
◉ www.earthisland.org

Earthwatch Institute
◉ earthwatch.org

International Union for Conservation of Nature
◉ www.iucn.org

Oceana
◉ na.oceana.org

The Nature Conservancy
◉ www.nature.org

UNEP-WCMC United Nations Environment Programme
◉ www.unep-wcmc.org

UNESCO United Nations Educational, Scientific and Cultural Organization
◉ en.unesco.org

WCS Wildlife Conservation Society
◉ www.wcs.org

WWF World Wide Fund for Nature
◉ www.worldwildlife.org

In the US:

AMNH American Museum of Natural History
◉ www.amnh.org

National Audubon Society
◉ www.audubon.org

NPCA National Park Conservation Association
◉ www.npca.org

NPS National Park Service
◉ www.nps.gov

SCA Student Conservation Association
◉ www.thesca.org

USGS United States Geological Survey
◉ www.usgs.gov

In Australia and New Zealand:

ACF Australian Conservation Foundation
◉ www.acfonline.org.au

Government of South Australia Department of Environment, Water and Natural Resources
◉ www.environment.sa.gov.au

NZ Department of Conservation
◉ www.doc.govt.nz

Parks Australia
◉ www.parksaustralia.gov.au

In the UK:

BSBI Botanical Society of the British Isles
◉ www.bsbi.org.uk

Friends of the Earth
◉ www.foe.co.uk

Greenpeace
◉ www.greenpeace.org.uk

JNCC Joint Nature Conservation Committee
◉ www.jncc.defra.gov.uk

The National Trust
◉ www.nationaltrust.org.uk

RSPB Royal Society for the Protection of Birds
◉ www.rspb.org.uk

The Wildlife Trusts
◉ www.wildlifetrusts.org